Babyhood

Also by Paul Reiser

Couplehood

Babyhood

Paul Reiser

ROB WEISBACH BOOKS

WILLIAM MORROW AND COMPANY, INC.   NEW YORK

Published by Rob Weisbach Books
An Imprint of William Morrow and Company, Inc.
1350 Avenue of the Americas, New York, N.Y. 10019

It is the policy of William Morrow and Company, Inc., and its imprints and
affiliates, recognizing the importance of preserving what has been written,
to print the books we publish on acid-free paper, and we exert our best
efforts to that end.

Library of Congress Cataloging-in-Publication Data has been applied for.

ISBN 0-688-14979-0

Printed in the United States of America

First Edition

1   2   3   4   5   6   7   8   9   10

BOOK DESIGN BY RENATO STANISIC

To Ezra Samuel Reiser,
the Boy of my Dreams.

And to his beautiful mother,
the Woman of those very same dreams.

(What did you think, I'd forget?)

And to my parents, with all the love in the world.
I think I get it now.

Contents

Author's Note

Every book I've ever picked up about babies seems to wrestle with the *pronoun* issue: Should it be "him" or "her," "he" or "she"? Are they writing about a baby boy or a baby girl?

It's not an insignificant dilemma. If you use just one gender, you could alienate half the readers. If you use the combination "he or she," you irritate *everybody*.

Some try to alternate usage, as in, "When *his* baby teeth first come in, *she* may show signs of fever."

This helps nobody.

The real diplomats use the baby-book version of Ms.—"s/he"—which, ultimately, means nothing. It's not even a word; it's just "he" with a slash and an alternative "s" standing by just in case. Basically, they give you all the letters, you pick the ones you want. It's a nice idea, but in practice, it's too hard. Plus, no one knows how to say it. Is it "sss-he," or "shhhhhh-he," or "she-*slash*-he"? Who wants that kind of aggravation?

The only real solution would be to customize each book with your very own child's name throughout the text. This way, even the most technical information becomes warm and fuzzy. For example:

Don't be alarmed if ***Dustin's*** umbilical stump becomes inflamed. This is very common, and can be treated easily by lubricating ***Dustin's*** inflamed stump with ***Dustin's*** favorite ointment.

But frankly, we're not set up for that kind of thing.

So I've decided to settle it this way: *I* have a boy, so the *book* has a boy. On every page, it's going to say "he" or "him."

Now, if *you* also have a boy, you should have no problem. You may begin.

If, however, you have a *girl*, please feel free to go through the book with a pencil and scribble in "s" or "her" wherever you see fit. But please, don't change any other stuff. I've worked very hard on it, and I would be upset if I ever came to your house and saw you messing up my book.

Thank you.

—P.R.

Los Angeles

Babyhood

In the Beginning

Okay, so here's what happened.

We're on a plane, my lovely wife and myself, sipping a tasty beverage, eating as many really salty nuts as we feel like, enjoying a perfectly bad movie together—in short, having a grand old time.

We had been married several years, gone through the rosy early parts, through all the scary stuff that comes immediately *after* rosy, and navigated ourselves successfully through enough little ups and downs to land on our feet and know with confidence that we were very good together and very much in love. Life was very nice.

So we're on this plane, and across the aisle from us was another couple, about our age, traveling with their two children—a two-year-old girl and a very new boy who, though tiny in stature, had a crying scream so piercing, it was annoying people on other planes.

The parents looked like hell. No kidding, they just looked like life had taken them by the ears and twirled them violently around in circles until finally, exhausted, weakened, and drained of even the capacity to *imagine* joy, they were flung into the seats next to us.

The little girl was running up and down the aisle, tripping on people's luggage, screaming when anybody talked to her, and screaming a tad louder when everyone tried to ignore her and *not* talk to her. The baby was wailing literally without pause from the Redwood Forest to the Gulf Stream Waters.

Somewhere over the midwestern states, the two-year-old took a couple of bites of airline macaroni—and then reconsidered, shooting the remains quite dramatically onto her daddy's jacket.

The mom, whose hair was graying before our eyes and caked with baby spittle and something else puddinglike, was spending the last of her waning energy trying to shield her eyes from her squirming infant's fast-flying fists.

When not occupied roping in their children or apologizing to the growing numbers of irritated passengers around them, the Dad was busy either bending or reaching to find one of a truly frightening number of carry-on bags, collapsible strollers, fuzzy toys, and assorted burdensome baby paraphernalia.

There was virtually no conversation between the two adults. What words *were* spoken were in the form of barked orders, desperate pleas for help, and bitter assignments of blame.

"Why are you letting her eat that?"

"I didn't."

"What—she opened the jar of macadamia nuts herself?"

"No, she must have gotten it from the—"

"Just take it from her."

"I *will*, if you just give me a second here . . ."

My wife and I, plastic champagne cups in hand, watched this circus for a good long while, then turned to each other and simultaneously said, "May the Lord protect us from ever becoming *that*."

Now, lest you think us unkind, let me point out that we're actually very nice people. And, in fact, we had always planned to have kids ourselves someday. Not Today, and not necessarily Tomorrow, but definitely Someday.

However, as we observed these people, we had all the reason we needed to push Someday back even *later* on the schedule. Watching this unfortunate display, all I could think was "Why? Why do that to ourselves?" Now that we had finally figured out how to successfully live together as *two* people, why would we want to jeopardize everything with a whole new human being for whom we'd be responsible every moment of every day for many, many years? I mean, the Couple Dance is tricky enough—dancing as a threesome would have to be impossible.

Three has *always* been tougher than Two. Think of any of your famous threesomes. The Three Stooges? Look at the anger *there*. My bet is that before Curly was born, Moe and Larry could play together for hours without even a single poke in the eye. Huey, Dewey, and Louie? Donald Duck never had a moment's peace. The Good, the Bad, and the Ugly? I rest my case.

Over the years, my wife and I had each argued convincingly every reason both *for* and *against* starting a family, but had somehow managed never to share the same opinion on the same day.

"What if we want to travel?"

"You can travel with kids," I would counter.

"Not to Africa."

"Who's going to Africa?"

"I'm just saying, hypothetically. What if we wanted to pick up and go to Africa?"

"Do you *want* to go to Africa?"

"Not particularly."

"So?"

"But, someday, I *might* . . ."

The problem with this type of argument is that on closer inspection, when you list all the things you fear you'd have to give up if you had a kid, you can't help but notice it's actually a pretty pitiful list.

"What else? What specifically are you afraid you're not going to be able to do with a kid that you do now?"

"Okay—sleep?"

"Fine. Are we really going to forgo being parents so we can nap?"

"Maybe . . . And what about going to the movies?"

"You can still go to the movies with kids."

"Yeah, but not whenever I *want*."

This is where the argument starts to crumble: When you realize you would consider not having a child just so you could take an occasional snooze and be available to see *Batman Retires* the same weekend it comes out, you have to take a good hard look at yourself and acknowledge, "I am a shallow, shallow person."

Which, if you need it, can be a perfectly valid reason for the "against" team.

"Hey, *we* can't have kids—we're too shallow."

On the other hand—batting for the "maybe we *should* have kids" team—we both saw the appeal in creating an entire new person who would be, in essence, a tiny "us." We spent a lot of time deciding which features of ours we'd want to pass down, which ones would be better off to skip. We started engineering the ideal combinations.

"Your eyes, my nose."

"My teeth, your ears."

"Your feet, my wrists."

You become like mad German scientists, though without the genocide and blatant disregard of other countries' borders.

You do, however, step on unforeseen land mines.

"*Your* hair, *my* gums."

"What's the matter with my gums?"

"Nothing. Okay, *your* gums, my nose, your lips, your laugh."

"Your voice."

"My toes."

"Really?"

"Yeah, because *your* toes do a funny thing—how the second one sort of drapes over the big one."

"So?"

"So, nothing, on *you* it's cute. It's a trademark. I wouldn't dream of taking it away from you. But as long as we're starting from scratch, why saddle a kid with that kind of thing?"

"Fine."

"So, my toes, your skin—"

"And numbers. I'm good with numbers, he could have that."

"And my enthusiasm for soups."

"Deal?"

"Deal."

At one point the lady with the kids noticed us staring. I got embarrassed and turned back to my in-flight magazine, which had an article on squirrels. (When you're on a plane, you start caring about things you ordinarily wouldn't.)

My wife, on the other hand, who is much nicer and can be—when she has to be—more mature, smiled and struck up a conversation.

"Your baby is just beautiful."

The woman was visibly moved.

"Thank you . . . I hope we haven't made too much of a ruckus . . ."

"No, not at all."

My wife can also *lie* more convincingly than most people I know.

"Do you have kids yourself?"

"No, but we've been thinking about it . . ."

Which wasn't really a lie, but didn't reflect the larger truth: We were thinking about it now only because the woeful reality that this woman and her husband called their "life" had all but convinced us to spend our years childless.

The woman smiled.

"You know, a few years ago, we were exactly like you. We used to get on a plane and pray we wouldn't sit near anyone with kids."

"Oh, we don't mind sitting next to kids," my wife said defensively. "We *love* kids."

"Hey, you don't have to pretend. I understand. But things change. You'll see. Before we had—"

WHAAPP!

The sound of her daughter's head slamming into the coffee cart brought the conversation to a halt. And as the woman dealt with this newest emergency, my wife turned back to me and pulled my headphones off my head.

"She thinks we don't like her."

"Why?"

" 'Why?' Because you were staring at her."

We looked over, guilt-ridden, and saw this woman, who was now less of a cartoon show and more of a real person, as she held her daughter in her lap and kissed the child's freshly bumped head.

"That's so sweet . . . ," says my bride.

"Mm-hmm. Very sweet."

"I want to have kids," she says.

"Hey, who said different?"

"But not right away."

"No, I know. We'll *have* kids, but when we're *ready*."

"Right . . ."

Beat.

"But I don't want to wait *too* long . . ."

"No, we won't," I assured her. "We'll wait, like, you know . . . just the right amount of time."

I'm well aware that not everybody gives the if-and-when of having kids this much time and deliberation.

A lot of people have kids who, frankly, didn't mean to.

Many people choose to have no kids at all and live quite happily.

But most people have kids simply because you're "supposed to." The rule book says once you get married, start churning 'em out. It's just "the next step," part of that nonstop momentum that keeps us all sprinting through life.

If you're a young single person and you meet someone you like, why not *take the next step*? Go out with them.

Of course, you can do that only so long before it's time to—*take the next step*. Get engaged. Get married. And no sooner do you become Man and Wife than everybody in the world starts giving you that annoying smile-with-a-head-nod that says, "So? When are you *taking the next step*?"

We constantly up the ante. We're a species that just can't leave well enough alone. *Animals* don't have this problem. You never hear snakes say, "Ideally, we'd like two girls and a boy."

They just do it. They procreate because that's simply what you do. They know that if they don't perpetuate their own species, no one is going to do it *for* them. Especially snakes. Because, to be totally honest, no one is that thrilled about getting *more* snakes. Nobody. You, me, other animals—no one walks around thinking, "Snakes. Boy, we need to send out for more of *them*." Snakes, therefore, must take very seriously upon themselves the business of making baby snakes.

We, however, can't claim to be having babies for the sheer survival of the species. There's no real shortage of humans out there. We're not doing it for mankind. We're doing it for ourselves.

And it's not even for a specific purpose. Like years ago, when families needed kids to work the farm. Most people I know pushing strollers aren't doing it because they need strong-backed young 'uns to work the soil. It's much more self-centered than that. We want to have kids for *us*. We believe that children will make us "complete"; they will make us whole.

Plus, we want someone to drive us around when we're old and nasty.

This is a big motivation for a lot of people.

"Even if we don't necessarily want a kid right now, we *are* going to want someone to take care of us in our golden years, and if we don't hurry, we're going to be driven around by, at best, a nine-year-old."

It becomes a matter of *which* self-centered impulse you want to service; the need to be free and unencumbered *now*, or the need to secure yourself a caretaker to whom you can be a huge encumbrance *later*.

"Let's see . . . we're going to need someone to put our things in order, someone to take all our junk when we die, and someone to take care of us and worry about us *before* we die . . . I don't know anybody who's going to do *that* . . . I know—let's *make* someone. Let's manufacture a whole new person, and then that'll be their job."

Then the thinking becomes, "Well, what about after we die? We don't want this kid to be alone, do we? I know—let's make *another* kid, for the sake of the first kid." And what kid wouldn't like *that* distinction?

"You're our first child—we wanted *you*. On the other hand, you, our *second* child—you're pretty much the spare."

The inevitability of old age forces you to do The Baby Math.

"Okay, so if we got pregnant right now, I'd be forty when the kid is born, which means . . . let's see . . . when I'm *sixty,* they'll still be in college . . . when they start a family of their own, I'm almost seventy, and if they wait even a *couple* of years to have their first kid, I'll be older than my grandfather was when he died . . . Okay, this is no good. It's too late. We missed it."

"It's the greatest thing in the world."

I had to take off my headphones again.

"I'm sorry?"

"I was just telling your wife—it's the greatest thing in the world. It's certainly not easy, and it does change your life forever, but it really is true: There is nothing more rewarding or wonderful than having children."

The best I could muster was a tiny smile and "That's what they say . . ."

New parents always sound like hucksters in a pyramid scheme. Anyone who has kids and then gets *you* to go and have kids gets a check from Huckster Headquarters. They're like newly converted religious fanatics, these people. They're not only hooked, but they won't rest till they bring *you* into the fold, too.

I smiled at the lady and put my headphones back on while pointing to the screen, as if to say, "I really would like to finish the conversation, but I tell you—this movie is just so darn funny . . ."

When the time came to get off the plane, we watched the exhausted new parents and their squawking progeny gather their belongings—which, together, was probably more than my grandparents packed to cross great oceans— and as we grabbed our We-Don't-Have-Any-Cares-in-the-World carry-on bags, the woman reached out, touched me on the arm, and said, "Good luck."

I remember thinking, "Hey . . . we're not the ones

who have to get a cab with fourteen hundred pounds of luggage. Good luck to *you*."

That night, we were getting ready for bed and brushing our teeth and still talking about those people on the plane.

"Did you see how pale they both looked?"

"I know . . . *both* of them . . ."

"Well, it's not exactly like you're going to the beach everyday when you've got little kids like that . . ."

"Hey, no kidding . . ."

We got into bed.

"Also keep in mind, they're older than us."

"Yeah, plus that's their *second* kid."

"Right."

"If we have a second kid, I'd definitely want to wait longer than they did . . ."

"Definitely."

"Maybe three years. At least . . ."

"Definitely . . . and, you know, there's no telling if we could even *get* pregnant right away. There's a very good chance it could take us a year or two for the *first* one . . ."

"I know, believe me, I've thought about that . . ."

Then there was a long pause.

"What the hell just happened?"

"I don't know."

"Have we decided anything here?"

"I'm not sure."

"I think we did. I think we were *snookered*. Those people snookered us . . . Didn't I tell you not to talk to those people?"

I tried in vain to trace the exact steps and conversations of the previous half day.

"I mean, we know we want to have kids *someday* . . ."

"Of course . . . we've never questioned *that* . . ."

"So what happened?"

"Maybe it's just time."

For several moments, nobody said anything. Then I jumped in.

"Yeah, but we don't really have any *values.*"

"Huh?"

"When you have kids, you're supposed to be able to teach them *values,* instill them with all your *values* . . . I don't know if I have any *values* . . ."

"You have values," my wife assured me.

"Do I?"

"Sure you do. You do unto others nicely, you never steal, you're polite to people from other countries . . ."

"Yeah, remember that time I gave those really long directions to that family from Canada? I didn't have to do that . . ."

"There ya go."

"Yeah, maybe you're right . . ."

It was very dark, and all I heard was my heart beating in my ears.

"So we're doing this?"

"What?"

"We're going to try to have a baby?"

A brief, sharp noise came out of my wife's throat—somewhere between a laugh and a squeal.

"It's not like it's going to happen overnight, you know . . ."

"No, I know . . ."

We looked each other firmly in the eyes.

"Are you telling me we're having a kid because a lady on a plane said something over Cleveland?"

"Yeah."

"It makes no sense."

"I know."

"So . . . you wanna try?"

"Yeah. Let's try."

We made an elaborate ceremony out of retiring all birth control paraphernalia (or, as a friend of mine so delicately puts it, "We yanked the goalie off the ice") and jumped back into bed.

We laughed and hugged and giggled and kissed.

And proceeded to not have sex for two and a half months.

The Big White Elephant

Once sex is for real, and not just for entertainment purposes, it's a much scarier proposition.

So even though we had both officially *committed* to procreating, we weren't actually doing anything about it. In fact, we were too scared to even talk about it. Sex became the proverbial Big White Elephant in the room that everyone sees and pretends isn't there.

Finally my wife suggested, "Look, we'll just be casual about it."

"Good idea . . . casual . . . we'll just see what happens."

"Yeah, we're not trying to get pregnant so much as we're *not* trying *not* to get pregnant."

Which is not exactly a vote of confidence for your child down the road.

"We wanted you more than anything in the world . . . but we could have skipped it, too."

Looking back, I think I know why we were hedging our bet: If it turned out we couldn't get pregnant, this seeming indifference might make us a little less devastated.

And also, there's this: As happy as you may be, when it comes to relationships, having a kid is the last level of *commitment.*

If you break up with someone you're living with, it's painful, it's heartbreaking, but let's face it: You lose some books, a spatula, some CDs, get a depressing apartment, and it's over.

If you get a divorce, it's *more* painful and *more* heart-breaking, you lose *more* books, *more* kitchenware, and *more* CDs, but, facing it once again, you sell your wedding ring, get one of those depressing *furnished* apartments, and *that's* over.

But if you have children, after all the pain and divvying up of material possessions, it ain't *ever* over. You could move to opposite sides of the universe, but you will, in the most physical and intimate of ways, be forever connected.

Fortunately for the human race, God is a very clever person. You see, by designing it so that the very act of reproduction feels, generally speaking, pretty good, it becomes inevitable that people are going to partake. People tend to like things that feel pretty good. Research shows that the activities involved in making babies are among the most popular, with all key age groups, in all major markets. Furthermore, the majority of people who've *tried* sex said they'd "like to try it *again*."

You have to admire the forethought. Had, for example, the Almighty-and-All-Powerful instead made sex an act of sheer pain and humiliation, how many people would have gotten involved? Not everybody. If our parents had to, let's say, slap each other in the head with enormous planks of linoleum and crawl hands-and-knees through acres of muddy stink to create Life, I don't know that we'd all be here today. But by shrewdly linking procreation to an act likely to make you stupid with excitement, God has seen to it that Life does indeed go on.

(It's possible, by the way, that this is why God's name comes up so often in the middle of the act; it's a salute to the author: "Hey, whoever made this up—thanks.")

So, sooner or later, even the most ambivalent of us get worn down by this divine cleverness. And to our pleasant surprise, this Sex for Real was really something. Without those spontaneity-killing trips to the medicine cabinet, there was suddenly a new sense of abandon, a certain devil-may-care flair that put an extra smile on everybody's face.

Sometimes you just have to say, "God bless God—He knows what He's doing."

Thank You for Sharing

My bride and I consider ourselves fairly private people. Between us, we have a handful of close friends who fall into three basic categories: She has a few close friends I don't really like; I have a few close friends *she* doesn't really like; and then, thankfully, we have those special few we *both* like.

Babyhood changed that.

Now we're suddenly on intimate terms with all sorts of people, including some people that, frankly, *neither* of us particularly like.

Once you start trying to get pregnant, the things you talk about with strangers will surprise you. We found ourselves comparing notes with couples we had never met before. Graphic descriptions of body parts and internal workings are exchanged as casually as directions to the airport.

"My breasts were so engorged I had to pump every two

hours, which, let me tell you—really cracked my nipples."

These are people who were simply invited to the same barbecue as us. We met over fruit salad.

But once people hear you're "trying," they just open up.

"Yeah, my wife and I are trying, too, but no luck yet. We tested my sperm, and Tuesday, my wife's getting her fallopian tubes Roto-Rootered, and then they're gonna look around for some of those *fibroids*. Hey, have you tasted this chicken? It's dynamite."

I certainly understand in *theory* that if you're going through an event as universal and wondrous as childbirth, and especially if you're having difficulties, there is benefit in sharing. But the reality is, I don't feel like discussing my genitalia with *anybody*.

Just *announcing* that you're trying seems awfully personal. You're basically telling anyone in earshot when, how, and why you're having sex. When did this become acceptable? You certainly didn't do it *before* you were trying to get pregnant. If you weren't specifically trying to conceive, would you stand up at the Thanksgiving table to say, "Folks, just want to let you know—we're having sex, on the average, two to three times a week, mostly in the missionary position—pass the cranberries?" No. You'd look like an idiot. But by merely having pregnancy as a goal, the lines of discretion and propriety are totally redrawn. You can, and are expected to, share everything.

And, of course, you then have to provide constant *updates*.

"So how's it going *now*? Have you had any success with the sex you two are having? 'Cause I *know* you're doing it—you mentioned it at Thanksgiving. I guess what I'm asking is, how *much* are you doing it? For example, did you do it *today*? How'd your sex go *today*?"

People want to be part of this pending miracle. Unfortunately, there's a very fine line between "So, when's the good news?" and "What's taking you guys so long?" Because the subtext there is "So, *one* of you seems to have a medical problem. Am I right? Is something wrong with one or more of you medically, physically, emotionally . . . ? Huh? Huh? Is there? You can tell *me* . . ."

There does seem to be at least a modicum of diplomacy in this area. Couples who *are* having difficulties conceiving generally close ranks and present one united front, so as to protect the feelings of the one whose body is indeed being uncooperative. They stand behind the generic "We."

"We're doing a few tests."

"We're trying some new drugs."

"We don't want to talk about it anymore."

Rarely will you hear a guy say, "We *wanted* to have children, but the wife here is just *barren*."

And even *more* rarely will they voluntarily take the heat themselves.

"The problem is—I have dead sperm. My testicles are unwieldy, and my sperm is just dead, dead, dead."

When you're trying to get pregnant, you both take a veritable crash course in biology and anatomy. Names of procedures and body parts that were once faraway places on that big map in your doctor's office become second nature.

But for men, this transformation is even more remarkable, because before this, they knew next to *nothing*. Women at least have a familiarity with the subject. Men? It's remarkable—*sad*, but still remarkable—how little they know of the actual mechanics operating within women's bodies. The whole business is referred to simply as "Down There."

"Yeah, they did some tests down there . . . looked around, it's very fascinating what's going on down there . . ."

But once aboard that Pregnancy Train, the education accelerates, and men find themselves giddy with information they should have known in eleventh grade.

And a lot of them can't wait to use it. With very little provocation, the words "uterus," "placenta," and "vaginal" are popping in and out of conversations like hummingbirds. Ironically, it's not the guys you might expect, either. The kind of guys who in everyday speech talk incessantly and crudely about women's body parts are now too embarrassed to discuss the very same subjects in terms of actual anatomy. On the other hand, the kind of guy who excuses himself from a room when someone tells the joke about the hooker and the snorkel-mask is exactly the guy who is now most likely to kick off a conversation with, "My wife has what they call an *incompetent cervix,* but her clitoris was number one in the state."

The Power of a Two-Inch Paper Stick

During the period we were officially "trying," there were a few times when we *thought* we had succeeded. After experiencing one or more telling symptoms, my wife would come in with a very peculiar look on her face and report with absolute certainty, "I'm not sure, but I think, maybe, it's not impossible, or entirely out of the question, that I may be, potentially, pregnant."

To which the only appropriate response is, "Well . . . then . . . 'Yippee' . . . possibly."

To get just a tad more information, we would then take the next big step and get out the *home pregnancy kit.* What a nice feeling to know that your entire future will be decided by a two-inch paper stick.

Before this technology existed, it wasn't so easy. Hundreds of years ago, if a woman noticed her clothes were getting continually tighter and she felt frequently queasy and exhausted, she had no way of knowing for certain if she was pregnant or simply had eaten some bad boar. She had to settle for, "Well, I guess we'll know in nine moons, won't we?"

But now we simply soil a piece of litmus paper and sit quietly for a couple of minutes.

During those fateful minutes, I found myself trying to prepare for either outcome, readying every possible emotional response and lining them all up in a row, so on a moment's notice I could grab the right one. If it came out positive, I was ready with, "Oh-my-God-what-wonderful-news-this-is-so-exciting-and-wonderful." If things went the other way, I had "Damn-it!-What-do-we-have-to-do-to-get-pregnant?" equally loaded and set to go. And over in the corner of my brain, so as not to be too conspicuous, was the third and least noble alternative, "Okay-to-tell-you-the-truth-I'm-a-little-relieved." I was ready for anything.

After waiting the prescribed number of minutes, my wife investigated, double-checked and triple-checked, and then looked at me.

"Guess what color it is."

"I don't know."

"Guess."

"What color is 'pregnant'?"

"Blue."

"Okay . . . I'm going to take a wild guess here . . . is it . . . 'blue'?"

She thrust it out in front of me the way someone

would fan their cards if they had an unbeatable straight flush.

"Blue."

Sure enough, there was a distinct blueishness to it.

The stakes were just blatantly and boldly raised. It was then I realized that all the other times we thought "This is it" were just feeble little minor-league moments. Melodramatic dress rehearsals. *This* was the this that was *it*.

It reminded me of when I was a kid and used to think I heard someone breaking into our house. I would grab my baseball bat and, with the stealthiest of superspy cool, stalk the halls, looking to clobber the guy. Then one time, while casing the place with my Louisville Slugger in hand, I heard a *really* loud noise which made me think there *really, really* was someone in the house. I promptly threw down the bat and tore out of the house just a hair faster than lightning. You may *think* it's real, but when something comes along even *realer*, you understand that up till then, you were just playing around.

Though my wife and I were both very excited, I wasn't ready to start sending out birth announcements. Part of me didn't completely trust the test, and the rest of me was just really scared.

"You know, it may not definitely be true."

"What are you talking about?" she said.

"I'm just saying these things aren't always a hundred percent accurate."

"They're accurate."

"Yes, but not all the time. So, I mean, you *may* be pregnant, but . . ."

"I *am* pregnant."

"Yeah, no, I know, I'm not saying you're *not* . . ."

"The stick is *blue*."

"Yeah, but not by a *lot*."

She looked at me suspiciously. "Why are you doing this?"

"All I'm saying is, it's *barely* blue. It's a very *light* blue. Like 'sky blue.' Sort of 'bad rental tuxedo blue.' "

"This, pal, is what they call 'baby blue.' "

"But I think it's supposed to be *dark* blue. Like *navy* blue."

She took a deep breath, looked down at the paper stick, and then slowly back up at me. There was a shadow of doubt in the jury's mind.

"It's blue," she said, with a tiny pause after the "blue" that sounded like ". . . *isn't it?*"

She made an appointment to see the doctor the very next morning.

When she came home, I was on the phone. I looked up and eagerly mouthed the word, "So?"

She motioned that she'd tell me in a minute.

I needed to know.

"What'd he say?"

She smiled. "Get off the phone."

My stomach tightened, made a fist, and punched me in the kidneys. This could only be one thing. She wouldn't make me hang up to tell me there was *no* news.

"Are you pregnant?" I mouthed, wide-eyed in disbelief, still holding the phone to my ear.

"Hang up the phone and I will tell you."

"I-have-to-get-off-the-phone," I mumbled to *somebody*.

SLAM.

"Okay. Tell me."

She smiled a smile I had never seen.

"Yes."

All the reactions I had practiced did not prepare me for the one that actually came, which was an electrifying chill from head to toe, followed by a piercing connection between us—eye to eye and heart to heart—that shouted of Newness. A wonderful and sweet Newness that lovingly but decidedly drew a very clear line in our life together. On one side was everything we had ever been through before, and on the other, this moment on.

The Morning After

Though I couldn't have known it at the time, this news also signified another little change in our relationship. Specifically, it was, I realize now, the moment my wife took charge of the whole thing.

The moment she walked in the door and informed me that *she* was pregnant and *we* were going to have a baby, she inaugurated the next phase of our relationship—and the one that, as of this writing, we're still in—the phase in which *she* has all the information.

Since that day, I don't think I have once told her anything she didn't already know. Nor, come to think of it, have I even found out anything *at the same time* she did. She gets everything first. By virtue of her body being Ground Zero for all pregnancy bulletins, and by virtue of her maternal instincts and accumulated knowledge, it has been my job to keep up with *her*, or, as has been much more often the case, find out from her in the first place that there already *are* things I have to catch up on. All because *she* broke the news to *me*. If, on the other hand, *men* got to announce the pregnancy, things might be different.

"Honey, sit down . . . there's something you should know . . . I've given this a lot of thought . . . after looking at your belly, and speaking to a lot of people I know who know things, I'm happy to inform you—and you're the first one I'm telling—you're pregnant!"

"Oh, Johnny—is that really true?"

"You bet it is, baby."

You'd look pret-ty clever, wouldn't you?

In the days that followed, I walked around with this wonderful sort of otherworldly buzz. There was not only exciting and terrific news to savor, but, since we had agreed not to share the news with anyone for at least a while, there was also a fun cloak of secrecy surrounding the whole thing. For probably the first time since we met, we had a *secret* to share that, devoid of any interfering input from anyone, bonded us solidly in our private, giddy enterprise. There were silly phone calls for no reason.

"Did you tell anyone?"

"No. You?"

"Nope."

"Swear?"

"Not a soul."

"I bought a rattle."

"Get out of here."

"Well, I didn't actually *buy* it, but I went into a store and I played around with one."

"Did you think of any names?"

"Many."

"Tell me."

"Okay, and I really like it . . . Roquefort."

"I gotta go."

I became fiercely protective of my wife and the amoeba of a child she was carrying. When we walked around outside, I was like a Secret Service guy, eyes darting everywhere, scanning the terrain for anything that smacked of trouble: a door that could open and swing into her belly, a sidewalk crack that could throw her off balance, an air-conditioner draft that might adversely overcool our incubating Loved One. I was bristling with energy and teeming with purpose.

The world had shifted, and everything around me glistened with new dimension. Every place I looked I saw a great place to be somebody's parent.

"I could walk into *that* 7-Eleven and buy my kid a soda . . . I could play ball in *that* park and teach my kid how to hit a jump shot . . . I could pass *that* statue and explain to my kid why Bolivia sent us a guy on a horse . . ." It all seemed nothing but good.

And, I must say, the knowledge that I had physically generated a new life was a surprising additional kick. I mean, I had, for many years, understood the mechanics of reproduction, and as a relatively healthy male, suspected I probably had it within me to contribute in this arena. But to have confirmation, validation, living, breathing proof—this was a great sense of power. My walk changed. I'd make my way across the very same parking lot I crossed every day, but now with a perceptible *strut*. I had, after all, successfully fulfilled the most basic and sacred function of my gender: I had "spread my seed." I had "spawned." I had "gone forth and been fruitful." Fruit was coming forth. My loins were bountiful. I was invincible. I was—*dun da dun*—"Fertile-Man."

It was an intoxicating feeling. I felt the urge to brag to strangers.

"I have produced a child, how-are-ya-nice-to-see-ya."

"Pardon me, we've never met, but I just wanted you to know I've procreated. Have a pleasant afternoon."

I had to stop myself from approaching women on the street. It was embarrassing.

"Excuse me, have you considered childbearing? Because if you're interested, I could help you create Life right now. No disrespect intended . . . nothing lecherous or lascivious about it—I'm simply here to assist. Because, you see—I am Fertile-Man."

No question about it, life was buzzing now. The clock was ticking and every tick brought excitement and adventure. It was somewhere around here that we both realized, "Okay, great, but we don't have the slightest idea what we're doing."

Every Day, Every Day
I Buy a Book

Books—in case you're not familiar—have things all written out for you, nice and legibly, that explain almost anything you want to know. So, to calm ourselves down, and to give us some specific outlet for our nervous energy, the mother-of-my-child-to-be and I went down to the nearest bookstore and hit those Baby Shelves. This is one of those sections of the store that, when you're *not* expecting a baby, you instinctively avoid. Like foreign language instructions in a VCR manual; nothing wrong with it, just clearly not for you. But suddenly, this section is your best friend.

You cannot believe how many books they have. There's not one phase or aspect of baby development that has not been thoroughly documented between covers. And each one seems an absolute must to read. Or at least a must to *buy*.

I'm not sure when this explosion happened. When we were babies, there was really only one book: Dr. Spock's *Baby and Child Care*. Between that and whatever they learned from *their* parents, our parents seemed to have everything covered. And what they didn't know, they made up as they went along.

But now there are thousands of choices, and one designed for everyone in the family. There's *Mother and Baby, Father and Baby, Grandparent and Baby, Baby and Whoever You Get to Stay with the Kid While You're Reading All These Books* . . . (And one of my favorites, *A Baby Is Born*, which they also made into a terrific movie with Barbra Streisand and Baby Huey.)

And the *titles* try desperately to outreach the competition. *Pregnancy and Birth* is shoved aside by **Conception**, *Pregnancy, and Birth*, followed by **Fooling Around,** *Conception, Pregnancy, and Birth*, and **Talking to Boys in the First Place,** *Fooling Around, Conception, Pregnancy, and Birth*.

These books don't just present information, they *demand* to be read. The titles *dare* you to pass them by. *Everything You Need to Know* . . . , *What You Really Must Know* . . . , *What Everyone Else Knows and Secretly Ridicules You Behind Your Back for Not Knowing* . . . There's never anything casual about it. You never see a book called *Only If You're Really Interested* . . . , *Well, If You Really **Must** Know* . . . , or *Frankly, This Probably Won't Come Up, But* . . .

I suppose I should appreciate that I live in a time when all this information is available. In the Middle Ages, for example, these kinds of books involved a lot more guess-work.

"Question: My child has a strange rattling sound in her chest. Is it demons?"

"Answer: Could be demons, could be an imbalance of bodily humours. Try applying leeches, administer a cupping, then sacrifice a newborn calf to Yahweh."

As we paid for our books—we ended up getting only two books that day, *What to Expect When You're Expecting* and *What to Expect When You're Expecting Not So Much a Baby but a Package from U.P.S.*—I felt very reassured.

"All right, so good . . . we'll take the books home, we'll read the books, and we'll know, more or less, what to expect."

"We'll be fine," concurred my bride.

Truthfully? I didn't read any of them. I glanced at 'em, but I can't honestly report that I read them. I *wanted* to, it's just that between the books *you* buy and the books you get as gifts and the ones dropped off by your friends whose kids are older now and need shelf space, it's just too much *book*. I was overwhelmed with books. (By the way, those hand-me-down books are extraspecial, because all the stains and dribbles found in the dog-eared pages have transformed them into unintentional "scratch and sniff" books. In addition to facts and graphs and pictures, you also get to find out what food your nephew was eating and during which chapter.)

My wife, on the other hand, read them all, and called me over when something caught her eye.

"Look at this."

"What?"

"Read that, right there."

" ' . . . this condition is known as *explosive diarrhea* . . . ' Jesus! Can that be true?"

"That's what it says . . ."

"This is exactly why I don't read these books."

To cover for my self-imposed ignorance, I took the position that this baby-book blackout reflected some sort of active core belief system.

"Personally, I find these books to be too theoretical, and to my way of thinking, there's just no substitute for hands-on experience."

Which sounds a heckuva lot better than "I was *gonna* read them, but there was a *Dick Van Dyke Show* on I never saw . . ."

Peanut Butter and
Lamb Chops

Even without reading any "What to Expect" books, there are *some* things everyone knows to expect. You know, for example, from every old movie, TV show, joke, and established cliché that pregnant women are likely to crave peculiar foods and have unpredictable mood swings. But when you go through it yourself, you still can't believe what's going on.

One time, only a few weeks into pregnancy, I was awakened in the middle of the night to the sound of muted sniffling and the gentle smacking of pasty lips. Now, if it had been the lip-smacking *alone*, I would have assumed it was the dog, once again licking himself grotesquely and thoroughly. But the *sniffling* was new. The dog, while certainly a loving and sensitive animal, had never actually been moved to tears. I turned over to discover my wife sitting up and staring into space.

"You okay?"

"Mm-hmm."

"You sure?"

She said, "Ask me what I did from two-thirty to now."

"Okay. What?"

"Ate a banana and cried."

Okay. That was a sentence I had literally never heard. To my knowledge, eating a banana and crying is something you would do only if you were, say, auditioning for a part in a dramatic monkey movie.

I didn't know exactly what to say.

"Why are you crying?"

"I don't know."

"You want to talk?"

"No."

A few moments of silence.

"Do you want me to get you anything?"

"No, I'm so nauseous."

"How many bananas did you have?"

"Eight."

"Well," I thought to myself. "There you go. That might be part of the problem." But something told me it would have been woefully unproductive to say, "Honey, next time, maybe don't eat so many bananas at one time." Instead, I extended myself as lovingly and unconditionally as I knew how.

"Is there anything I can do for you?"

"Yeah—shut up and leave me alone."

.   .   .

This particular fun patch of your couplehood presents some of the juiciest, trickiest, and most explosive mine-fields that you will encounter in your linked-together little lives. Nowhere is a loving husband's ability to tap-dance, turn the other cheek, and "just walk away" put more relentlessly to the test.

The key to survival, I found, was in accepting that virtually nothing I did would be right. And if I *did* do something right, it was probably by accident. I reminded myself constantly that whatever horrific outbursts she unleashed, however vicious the attacks that came my way, they were all the result of tsunami-sized waves of surging hormones and should not reflect unnecessarily harshly on the Woman I Love. Until this phase blew over, I would just shake off these blows, pick myself up from the canvas, and again politely offer her my chin.

I think most husbands accept this pretty readily, because even the dumbest of the group knows that they're still getting off pretty easy. After all, it's not *their* bodies going through these violent upheavals.

I remember one night I felt my wife's head and was concerned she might be getting a fever.

"Gee, you seem hot," I said in an irrefutably sympathetic tone.

Her response?

"Yeah, maybe it's because I'm in @#*!#-ing *HELL*."

Apparently, that's not uncommon. When you're in @#*!#-ing hell, your forehead can feel a wee bit feverish. (By the way, that's the way my wife actually curses. She doesn't use dirty words; she'll literally say "asterisk, pound sign, exclamation point, the-letter-'A'-with-a-circle-around-it, asterisk, asterisk, asterisk.'')

I thought I was prepared for the food cravings. Having seen enough *I Love Lucy* reruns growing up, I was all set to run out, any time of day or night, for pickles and ice cream. As it turns out, my wife had no interest in either pickles *or* ice cream. However, we couldn't get our hands on enough peanut butter and lamb chops. Peanut butter and lamb chops—which was also, interestingly enough, the name of a delightful children's show I enjoyed as a young boy—were not foods that had ever been a significant part of our life before pregnancy. In fact, my wife almost never ate *either.*

So where did these cravings come from? I concluded it's the baby, *ordering in.* Prenatal takeout. Even without ever being in a restaurant, fetuses develop remarkably discerning palates, and they are not shy about demanding what they want. If they get a hankering, they just pick up that umbilical cord and call.

"You know what would taste good right now? A cheeseburger, large fries, and a vanilla shake. And if you could, hurry it up, because I'm supposed to grow lungs in a half hour."

In an ideal world, once you ascertain what it is your wife craves, you would stock up on it and have more ready at all times. In the *real* world, however, not only does the hankering change day to day and hour to hour, but the very same thing that hit the spot at one in the morning can be the most repulsive suggestion imaginable at one forty-five.

"I'm starving."

"How about another lamb chop?"

"Uchhh! What's the matter with you?!"

"What'd I say?"

"I'm going to throw up right in this chair."

"I thought lamb chops were helping."

"Stop!"

"What?"

"Stop saying it!"

"What—lamb chops?"

"Hey!"

"Sorry . . ."

It is virtually impossible to suggest the right snack to a pregnant woman. The chance of hitting the bull's-eye is infinitesimal, and, more significantly, the margin for error is enormous. As a reasonably intelligent person, I could pretty safely guess that if someone's feeling queasy, it's better not to suggest, let's say, a warm glass of *clam juice.* You just know that. Certain foods simply do not paint a pretty picture: Sweetbreads. Frog's legs. Sauerkraut soufflé. Crabmeat daiquiris . . . clearly all to be avoided. But— a *cracker?* Never would I have dreamed that the mere mention of a dry, salted *nothing* of a cracker could send a grown woman lunging for a sink. But I *did* mention it, and she *did* lunge.

In addition to the wild cravings and the crippling nausea, women also get the tougher end of the deal foodwise, because they have to restrict themselves in consideration of the youngster hatching within. A lot of nifty foods and delectable beverages are cut right out of the picture. Wonderful man that I am, I jumped behind my wife in full support.

"You know what, sweetie? If *you* can't have any wine, *I* won't have wine either. You can't have a sip of beer? None for me, then. No spicy food for you? I, too, shall abstain. I shall submit myself unwaveringly to the very same grueling regimen of denial and sacrifice as you, my love."

But after a while, I had to rethink it.

"Look, I know what I said, but let's be honest: *You* have to protect the well-being of our child. Me? I was just trying to be nice . . . There's no reason I should have to put myself through *that,* is there, really? I mean, not that I'm not enjoying the steamed bok choy and brussels sprouts platter, but I'm just going to grab a pepperoni pizza and seven beers. I will, however, eat over *there,* so don't worry, you won't see a thing . . ."

The one aspect of this whole food circus that I wish someone had told me about is how much weight *men* put on during pregnancy. Traditionally, dads-to-be pile on as much as—and often *more than*—the women who are actually With Child.

I'd like to say I did it on purpose. To "keep my wife company."

The sad truth is, I didn't know it was going on. It quietly snuck up on me. In retrospect, it shouldn't have been that surprising. Not only did I snack every time *she* snacked, but more often than not, I'd run down for some food that the Love of My Life needed to have *"NOW!!!"* and in the time it took me to prepare it just-to-her-liking and sprint it back upstairs, the aforementioned Love of My Life had changed her mind. The oh-so-urgent urge was no longer urging. And as I mentioned, not only is that very same food—ordered minutes ago—no longer desirable, it's now entirely *disgusting*. The thought that I would even be *holding* a plate and making it available is both repulsive and a testament to the enormity of my insensitivity.

So as I would head back down the stairs in conciliatory retreat, I'd think, "Well, *someone's* got to eat all this spaghetti . . ." And the next thing you know, there's twenty pounds of extra Person around the top of your pants that didn't use to be there.

And sadly, *men* going through pregnancy are never admired for the mass they accumulate. While everyone's lining up around the block to feel and revere my wife's expanding belly, nobody's applauding *me*. I'm part of this thing, too, you know . . . I think it would be nice if just once during the pregnancy someone came over to me and said, "That's a lovely gut you've got there. May I touch it?"

"Sure. Thanks for asking . . . and if you want to come back in a while, we're going to be having doughnuts and spareribs. Wait till you feel *that*."

"Y'Know What You *Have* to Get . . ."

Over the first few months of pregnancy, we watched other couples with babies and concluded that we not only had a lot of things to learn, but a lot of things to go out and *buy*. People with kids just accumulate an unbelievable amount of *stuff*. It's sort of like taking up a new sport. And I have always subscribed to the rule, "Whatever you lack in skill, make up for in silly accessories."

"How's your tennis game?"

"Not great, but I have a racket the size of an outdoor grill, the exact same sneakers as Agassi, and a hat with a tiny solar-powered fan that keeps me very cool."

I figure if they went to the trouble of manufacturing it, there's probably a very good reason. And I'd be crazy not to get one.

Especially where your child is concerned. Even if the

kid is still in the womb, you want to send the message that every conceivable comfort will be provided.

Sadly, I had no idea what I was up against. There's an infinite number of store chains, all with cutesy names that aim to convey both the smallness of babies and the enormity of their selection: "Tot Town," "Teeny World," "Infant Hemisphere," "All That's Small," "Papoose Palace," "Mess-O-Whipper Snappers." And they really are gigantic. The first time my bride and I ventured into one of these retail monsters, I got literally dizzy. Seriously, I had to lie down. The sheer size of these places is staggering. Three miles long, eight hundred aisles, each a building-and-a-half high—an unfathomable array of choices.

As we wandered down the first few miles of this store, we tried to familiarize ourselves with the inventory.

"Look at this—a diaper *genie* . . . "

"If you rub it and ask it to clean up the diapers, it has to do it?"

"I think so . . ."

"Okay . . . good . . . What's this—'Four-in-one car seat'?"

"It's a car seat, but the seat comes out and you carry the baby in the bucket part. So it's like a carrier, too."

"So, how is that 'four-in-one'?"

"Because you can also put it on the thing with wheels, and push the baby in the seat."

"Okay, so that's *three*."

"What?"

"That's only '*Three*-in-one.' "

"Yeah . . . so?"

"It says '*four*.' "

"Yeah . . . well, maybe they counted wrong."

We perused the next aisle.

"Why would you need a crib *and* a cradle?"

"The cradle is for the beginning, and then they move on to the crib."

It was becoming clear that my wife was further into the "Preparing Your Baby's Room" chapter than I was. I still had questions.

"How long do they sleep in the cradle?"

"I don't know . . . a few months?"

"And then what?"

"Crib."

"They don't go back to the cradle?"

"Why would they go *back* to the cradle?"

"I don't know . . . because we *have* it. It seems like a shame to get a whole cradle if they're only going use it for an hour and a half . . ."

"Maybe we don't need the cradle."

"That's all I'm saying."

In addition to cribs and cradles, you also have to consider playpens, which at first impression struck me as no more than brightly colored, miniature *jails*. Is this really how we want to treat a brand-new person? Poor thing spends nine months cooped up in the womb, and first thing we do is toss him in a cage like a zoo animal. At least zoo animals get shrubbery and little ponds and schoolchildren tossing them peanuts.

You can also, evidently, purchase a *porta-crib*—the beauty of which is that no matter where you may travel, your newborn gets to stare at the *same* four nylon walls.

"Okay, Junior, we're going over to visit the Millers, who have a beautiful house filled with lovely antiques and a stunning view of the mountains. But it doesn't really matter, because to you, it'll look just like every other place—a small purple rectangle."

(This, of course, assumes you can *assemble* the rectangle. When we later got one of these as a gift, I followed the instructions to the letter, but still ended up with some sort of post-modernistic sculpture/collage of plastic, metal, and mesh netting, which, while totally uninhabitable for infants, *is* currently on loan to the Guggenheim.)

The jewel in the baby product crown is the *stroller*. And if in America you are what you drive, then in Parentland, you are what you *push*. This department had its own salesman, and as soon as he saw us, the guy swooped down like a vulture in a bad tie.

"Hi, how are you two this afternoon?"

"Well, we're actually just looking."

"Of course . . . Well, you obviously have an eye for quality."

"We do?"

"Absolutely. *This* stroller you're looking at here is considered the Cadillac of strollers."

"Honey, did you know that strollers have a 'Cadillac'?"

"I didn't."

"Oh, yeah," the guy says. "Check out the wheelbase on this baby. And the plush interior. Your baby will be riding in the height of comfort and safety. Believe me, when people see you pushing this down the road, they'll say, 'Why, *there's* two people who really care about their child.' "

This is a guy with an easy job.

I don't imagine there are a lot of jobs *easier* than being a baby-store salesman, simply because you can't say no to them. You can't negotiate. If you walk into Planet Tinywood and a salesman tells you, "You don't *need* the high chair with the extrasafe support lock, but it *is* safer"—what are you going to say?

"Thank you, sir, but we're gamblers by nature and are curious to see if our infant doesn't do exactly as you predict and slide right out on his head, crashing violently onto the hardwood floor. That's something we'd like to see . . ."

And you can't believe how many different *types* of strollers they have. One for every conceivable occasion. You have your heavy-duty, everyday stroller; your pack-up-and-travel *umbrella* stroller; your "this-is-only-good-for-going-from-the-car-into-the-mall" stroller; and the very popular *jogger* stroller—which when I first saw I thought was pretty cool, but after having a child, I have come to view as more of an irritant. Because when you have a newborn, you realize, "Who has the energy to jog?"

It's my opinion that even *conceptually*, going from a "stroller" to a "jogger" is a move in the wrong direction. What we need is a "napper." A big Bed on Wheels, pulled by a team of hefty Akitas. *You* get to rest, the kid sees the world, and the dogs get walked—it's a win-win-win proposition.

And if I can be honest here, when I see someone actually jogging with their baby, I always feel the need to give the parent a little *smack*. Because if, after being up all night with your baby, you still have it in you to run around the neighborhood pushing something, I don't need to know about it. (And if you're so peppy, I see no reason why you couldn't accept one tiny little smack in the head from me.)

Ultimately, I say, "What kind of nut runs in the streets with a baby, anyway?" That can't be good. Even just walking, I always thought it kind of perverse that people push their kids into traffic *ahead* of them. The premise is, apparently, "If it turns out to be safe enough for the baby, I will then step forward myself." I think they should design a stroller you drag from *behind*, or one that attaches to your *side*, so at least you're *both* taking a risk.

But I digress.

Back in Youngster-burgh, we meandered through the first five or six acres of strollers and cribs and playpens without incident, and then came upon a section of stuff I never even knew about: baby exercise products. These contraptions are no doubt well intended, but seem like a cruel practical joke we play on the kids.

"We're not going to let *you* move around, but we will

bind you to a mechanical device which will give you the *illusion* of movement."

I couldn't believe how many ways there are for a baby to be strapped in, buckled up, fenced in, suspended, cradled, swung, hung, couched, supported, contorted, and held. But after enough time in the store, I figured out what it's all about; I isolated the simple premise on which this huge child-care/child-maintenance industry is based: The Baby's Buttocks. Everything they make is designed specifically to, in one way or another, accommodate the Butt of a Baby. You're either resting it, holding it, shaking it, cleaning it, or transporting it. Think about it: high chairs, baby baths, bassinets, playpens—all essentially different places to temporarily park your baby's rump. Johnny Jumpers, bouncy chairs, swingomatics, exersaucers—different ways to move it around. Changing tables, diapers, diaper covers, diaper genies, diaper hampers, diaper wipes—I think we know where the main focus of concern is here. And, of course, the plethora of car seats, strollers, backpacks, snugglies, infant carriers—all just trying to help you get your baby's ass from Here to There without ever touching the ground.

Once you go ahead and buy every piece of merchandise with the word "baby" in the name, you still have another problem: How do you get all this stuff home? The answer, of course: Get rid of your car and find yourself a big ugly four-wheel-drive/trucky/sport utility/"just-throw-everything-in-the-back" vehicle. Suddenly you understand those behemoth station wagons your parents had.

But because we are, as a group, so very much more clever, we now surround ourselves instead in hulking *tanks*—uglier by far than anything we sat in the back of when we were five. But this time they have much *cooler names*. Names reeking of adventure: Explorer, Expedition, Outback, Range Rover, Land Cruiser, Four Runner, Trooper, Pathfinder . . . Where do we think we're going? We're picking up diapers and dropping off a video. We're not bagging a cheetah and lugging it across Kenya.

And when you outgrow *these* cars, you next find yourself in a *mini-van,* the last stop down on the "I used to be cooler than this" slide. Because in a jeep, you can at least still *pretend* to be cool. When you're at a stoplight and an attractive woman pulls up alongside you, you can still smile and convince yourself, "Maybe she thinks I'm enormously rugged, and the car is loaded up with equipment for that very dangerous geological expedition."

But in a *mini-van*, you're fooling no one. You're on your way to Gymboree, the side compartments are stuffed with diaper wipes, and the interior is all sticky with apple juice.

You know what? You're not Indiana Jones; you're a dad.

And Thy Name
Shall Be . . . Something

Naming your child is a monumental responsibility. You get to tag and identify—for life—a whole new person. Throughout your child's life, it will come up every hour of every day.

"Name, please."

"Hi, what's your name?"

"Sorry, I didn't catch your name."

"We just need you to sign your name."

"Would you put last name first, first name last, middle initial . . ."

"May I ask who's calling?"

"Name and Social Security number . . ."

"Honey, guess who's on the phone?"

"You know who we haven't heard from in a while?"

"And the *name* of the deceased . . . ?"

And with every usage, that name—the result of hours

and hours of debate, and the consideration of an infinite number of variables, uninvited input, and conflicting personal agendas—that name will, for good or bad, represent to the world and its people, for all eternity, your child.

Which is why you don't want to screw it up.

People screw up their kids' names all the time. Not on purpose. In fact, usually with the best of intentions. The new parents who want their child to stand out and be recognized, who want more than anything to thrust their child forward from the sea of common and interchangeable surnames, are the ones responsible for kindergartens full of Zebadiahs, Queequegs, and Moons. Lovely and creative names all. Unfortunately, these kids are in for a lifetime of quizzical stares, judgmental smirks, and patronizing displays of phony interest, in response to which they can only say, "Yeah, my parents were into a thing . . ."

The power is extraordinary. The simple combination of letters and sounds *you select* can result in a life of carefree coolness or decades of expensive therapy.

"Hi, I'm Jake" versus "Hi, I'm . . . Tapioca."

Not to denigrate the virtues of being unique. It's just that there's a fine line between Good Unique and Just Plain Wrong. Good Unique is when you call your child's name and he's the only one who comes running. Just Plain Wrong is when they're running because they're being chased.

I imagine that part of the reason there are so many Bobs and Janes year after year is that even parents who *want* to be creative ultimately chicken out. And understandably.

You never know when the name you love today is going to be hideous tomorrow. The Ashleys, Dylans, and Maxes of our children could turn out to be what Hortense, Gertrude, and, frankly, Max were when *we* were growing up. It's sort of like the jacket you wore in your high school yearbook photo; it may have been cutting-edge that week, but for the rest of your life, you're "the maroon-plaid-jacket guy with lapels the size of sea flags."

Prior to this child, the only comparable experience we had was naming our dog—which is undeniably less complicated. There's no family lineage to protect, no concern for how it sounds followed by your last name . . . The only real question is, "How does it sound yelled across a park?"

Some pets, sadly, wind up never getting named at all. Who doesn't know a cat named Kitty or a dog named Dawg?

And if you can't come up with a great name deserving of their species, it's certainly acceptable to give your pet a People's Name. But rarely the reverse.

"Are you coming to Scruffy's piano recital? Oh, you really should . . . you know, *Snowball's* going to play the trombone."

You almost never hear that.

But when choosing a name for your child, there's a lot more at stake. The name-er can influence profoundly the life of the name-ee. Of course, it's hard to determine what's "nature" and what's "nurture"; does somebody turn out as they do *because* of their name, or do they *get* the name that's appropriate for the life they were on their way to living anyway? Hard to say. All I know is that if you name your daughter Trixie or Tina, she's more likely to sleep in a van with a band from Seattle than the exact same girl named Ruth. Similarly, a boy named Herbert *may* grow up to play baseball professionally, but not as easily as Dale, Pee Wee, or Scooter. This, of course, is not scientifically documented or anything, but . . . I think I know what I'm talking about.

A lot of people tell you that their kid popped into the world and the name just *revealed itself*.

"He looks like an 'Elliot.' Let's call him 'Elliot.'"

Come on—*nobody* seven minutes old looks like "Elliot." It takes *years* to look like "Elliot." (And interestingly enough, slightly less for "Neil" and "Howard.")

If they're like most newborns, your precious new one will enter this world looking like one of three things: Winston Churchill, Mahatma Gandhi, or a boiled chicken. That's basically it. (It *is* possible for a baby to look like Churchill or Gandhi *and* a boiled chicken, but this usually goes away with time and plenty of fluids.)

In some cultures they don't even name their babies right away. They wait until they see how the child develops; see what they do, see how they behave . . . and then name the kid accordingly. Like in *Dances with Wolves*. If you stand with your fists clenched, you're called Stands with a Fist. I like that system. It certainly makes it easy to remember people you've met.

"How's that guy doing?"

"What guy?"

"You know . . . *what's-his-name,* the guy who's always yelling at the vegetables . . ."

"Oh, you mean Barks at Salad?"

"Yes, yes, Barks at Salad . . . how's *he* doing? . . ."

Unfortunately, in *our* world, kids' names would be less romantic and poetic. Certainly less *warrior-like.*

"This is my oldest boy, Falls Off His Tricycle, his friend, Dribbles His Juice, and my beautiful daughter, Allergic to Nuts."

We bought every book out there on baby names, because when you're not by nature good with decisions, what could be more pleasant than slugging through the list of every name registered in every town on the globe? While it is nice to learn about other peoples, I'm not sure that any one family needs *that* many choices. You're probably going to stay within a given range. Very few people end up deciding, "Okay, so, Achmanzlebred if it's a girl, and if it's a boy—Scott."

You do, however, get to learn the etymology and origin of names, which is useful for parents trying to boost the self-esteem of kids stuck with *loser* names.

"Sweetheart, you know Milton *actually* means 'Ferocious Fighter of Freedom' . . ."

There was a period where our child's birth was getting really close, and we still had nothing. We were dangerously close to calling him Untitled Baby Project. The discussions intensified.

"You really don't like Penelope?"

"Really don't."

"Why?"

"I don't know. I just . . ."

"Come on . . . *Penny*. You like the name Penny, don't you?"

"I guess . . ."

"Sure you do . . . Penny *Marshall*, Penny *Lane* . . . Penny for Your *Thoughts* . . ."

"I don't have anything against Penny . . ."

"So? Penelope *is* Penny. It's the same thing."

"You *say* it's the same thing, but it's *not* . . . If it was so much the same thing, why would you have to shorten it? You're obviously dressing it up to try and sell it to me. Like, what—if you say Penny enough times, I'm going to forget the 'el-o-pee' is there? I still know it's there."

Certain names you eliminate not because there's anything wrong with the name, it just has a bad personal history.

"What's the matter with Merrill again?"

"That girl Merrill I knew in high school who ate egg salad through a straw."

"Oh, right . . . so we're crossing out Merrill."

"Please."

And some names you can *both* eliminate pretty comfortably.

"Adolf?"

"Out."

"Medusa?"

"Out."

"Tweety?"

"Let's talk about it for a second."

You see, some names may *sound* silly but prove to be advantageous in the real world. For example, the not-particularly-common-but-not-unheard-of Bumpy.

Now unless you're raising a Disney cartoon, you're probably not going to name your child Bumpy. It's silly, childish, and laughable. But isn't "laughable" potentially *good*? For example, how could anyone say no to a person named Bumpy? Think about it: You just got home, you had a terrible day, you don't want to see anybody, talk to anybody, think about anybody . . . The doorbell rings.

"Ah, geez . . . *Who is it?*"

"It's *me*—Bumpy."

Beat.

"Okay, come on in."

You're going to let the guy in.

"I hope you're by yourself."

"Well, I brought my cousin, *Blinky*."

"Ohhh . . . all right, both of you, come on in . . . but only for a little while."

Some people don't agonize at all about finding the perfect name. They simply give the kid *their* name.

"He'll be *me*, but Me *Junior*. To be followed by Me the Third, and *his* son, Me the Fourth."

Certainly moves things along. Of course, if you're *really* pressed for time, do what heavyweight champ George Foreman did—name all of his kids George Foreman.

God bless him, a great fighter, a fine humanitarian—not, apparently, the most creative in the naming department. An entire family named George Foreman. It's not like they're of successive generations, overlapping only here and there for a few years . . . No, this is almost half a dozen guys, with the exact same name, all living in the same house.

"This is my son George Foreman, his younger brother George Foreman . . . this one here is five and a half, say hello to George Foreman, and the little ones . . . where are they? . . . George Foreman? George Foreman? Come over here . . . okay, now, say hello, this is George Foreman and George Foreman . . . Why don't you all sit down on the couch over there—the couch, interestingly enough, I call George Foreman."

For others, the task of naming is simplified by family mandates. There are people to be honored and remembered.

"The child will be named after his grandfather." Or, "She will take her mother's surname, and it shall be as her own . . . And they shall go forth unto themselves, with their beasts and their grains, and into the desert shall they sojourn." (I'm sorry, I just saw *The Ten Commandments* on TV and frankly, I enjoy talking like that.)

In our case, we knew we wanted to name our child after my father. We didn't want to use the *exact* same name, but something beginning with the same letter. We had plenty of girls' names we liked, but nothing for a boy. Of course, when our son came out a boy (as almost all sons do) we were stuck. So we decided instead to honor my father's name by making it our son's *middle* name—which unfortunately has, to some, the tainted veneer of "second place." Middle names are kind of like vice presidents: It's a fine distinction and certainly an honor, but you're never not aware that someone else got the *real* job.

Parents often give middle names just so that later, when they're yelling at the kid, they can drag it out.

"Henry David Thoreau, you come in here this instant!"

It gives them something extra to sink their teeth into.

And a lot of people *have* middle names but you never know it. You can be friends with someone for years without ever once hearing their middle name. It becomes an area of unspoken intimacy, to be shared with only the select few.

If, however, you *assassinate* someone, your middle name is all over the place. Once you shoot a famous person, not only do you go to jail and sit alone hungering for a forgiveness that eludes you your whole life, but on top of that, your middle name, whether you like it or not, gets publicly and permanently cemented right between your first and last name. They just run those puppies together like Sonny-and-Cher. There's no way you can undo something like that.

But because of the potential anonymity enjoyed by middle names, they also represent opportunities for Name Givers to safely store their really creative choices. That way the name is *there*, but not everybody has to know about it. Unless you want them to. So when you meet kids named Stanley DiMaggio Miller or Carol Satchmo Smith, you know their parents had healthy doses of not only creative sparks but discretion, too.

The moment you announce your child's name, people take it in for a moment, digest it, and then say, "Okay, but what are you going to *call* him?"

"What do you mean, what are we going to call him? His name."

"No, of course, but what's the *nickname* going to be? I mean, *Franklin* is a beautiful name, but what do we call him? Frank? Frankie? Frankle? Frankfurter?"

This was a setback I hadn't seen coming. After finally landing on a name the two of you like, your family tells you it's not enough. You have to come up with a menu of officially sanctioned deviations and nicknames, which they're going to disregard anyway.

"Hello, Snooky . . . Hello, Angel-puss . . . Who's my sweet Pumpkin . . . ?"

They get called a lot of *foods,* these babies. "Pumpkin," "Angel Cake," "Cupcake," "Ducky," "Honey," "Sweet Potato," "Sweet Pea," "Sugarplum," "Peaches," "Pudding" . . .

But not *all* foods. You never hear someone call an infant "Steak." "Chicken Parmigiana." "Rice Cracker." "Eggs."

I think the rule of thumb is, desserts and side dishes are okay, entrées and appetizers, not okay. The only exceptions that I'm aware of are my Aunt Cutlet and Uncle Bisque, who were actually born with those names but, ironically, were later nicknamed Phyllis and Lloyd.

One Sonogram Says
a Thousand Words

From what I gather, seeing a gynecologist is not like seeing any other kind of doctor. It's more like seeing a Therapist Who Also Examines the Inner Reaches of Your Genitalia. Women *bond* with their gynecologists.

Men have none of this. You rarely hear men say, "I just *love* my proctologist." Or, "I really need a urologist I can *talk* to."

For women, though, this relationship is very complex. Among other considerations, the *gender* of their gynecologist can be a big issue. And often for men, too. Because these people are looking at other people's wives naked. And I know they're professional, and it's "just a job," but still, come on . . . women are coming in one after the other and taking their clothes off. Maybe I'm developmentally arrested, but that's gotta count as *something,* doesn't it?

And if these men *are* entirely professional, and view their patients solely as patients and not as Women, I would ask, "How come? Are you telling me my wife is sitting there naked and you don't even notice? I ought to slap you right here and now."

There's no way to win on this one. If you walked into a bar full of drunken gynecologists and overheard your wife's guy say, "You know who's really great looking . . ." and he started describing your wife, you probably wouldn't be happy. And if they went the other way and said, "I'll tell you who was *really* gorgeous . . ." and proceeded to talk about someone *not* your wife, you could get upset, too.

"What do you mean? Are you going to sit there and tell me your ten-forty-five appointment was cuter than my wife? You may have to get slapped yet again."

It turns out my wife's doctor was a very nice guy. Each visit began with the usual exchange of quasi-personal pleasantries—as if a perfunctory "Nice to see you, how's your dog?" would somehow distract from the fact that his forearm was disappearing into the woman I love.

Anytime the three of us were in the room together, it felt like only two of us could be a couple at one time. When he was examining and probing, I often felt like I was the intruder—despite his best efforts to include me.

"I do feel a slight inflammation in the lining of your wife's uterus."

"Thank you" was usually what I wound up saying,

followed by, "I think the two of you really need to be alone now."

Often, he would leave us momentarily to tend to other business, and my wife and I would return to being The Couple—a transition that always felt odd. We went from serious adults who were discussing matters of medical importance with this trained professional to suddenly being just a goofy couple in a room, one of whom was virtually naked and had just been handled in the most personal of ways, and the other of whom was standing there in a jacket. It usually made us silly.

"What do you think happens if I press this lever here?"

"Leave it."

"What's he going to do—yell at us?"

"Leave it."

I made great discoveries with the guy's stethoscope, placing it on various parts of my wife.

"Ooo, listen . . ."

"What?"

"Your capillaries are playing 'Mustang Sally.' "

"Shhh—put it down, here he is."

"So, Doctor, you're saying that these Braxton-Hicks contractions are entirely normal and nothing to worry about."

"That's correct. Wait a second, where's my stethoscope?"

"She took it."

.   .   .

Our favorite part of these visits was when we got to see the sonogram. If there's any event in the pregnancy that reminds you something real is going on, the sonogram is it.

The first time we saw the wavy image of our child we were ecstatic. We took the little printout and showed it around town like it was a Van Gogh.

"Look at that . . . we *made* that."

We looked forward to each subsequent sonogram like it was our favorite show. We'd dim the lights, pull up our chairs, pull up our stirrups, and settle in for the latest installment of *My Little Fetus*. The reception wasn't that great, but the show had everything: When the little guy turned to the camera and thumbed his nose at us, we had comedy. And when the doctor momentarily couldn't find our child's heartbeat, we had one brief but terrifying moment of drama.

The show even had mystery: Is there or is there not a penis?

My bride and I decided early on to let the sex of our child be a surprise. We figured we had all our lives to know the sex. And once we knew it, it's not like we were going to forget it. So why not try *not* knowing for a while.

Plus, we'd heard horror stories of parents who were mistakenly told their child was a boy, got all set for a boy, bought boy clothes and boy toys, and then, in fact, had a girl. And since it was too late to return everything, they had to *raise* her as a boy anyway.

While we appreciated the doctor and his staff for respecting our wish not to know, we also got a kick out of watching them trip all over themselves as they struggled to speak in gender-neutral pronouns.

"You'll notice that those are its feet and those are its arms . . . Yes, this sure is a beautiful little . . . *person*."

We also had fun looking for early traces of family resemblance.

"Gee, honey, it looks just like your mother, if she were small, bald, had no eyelids, and was floating in amniotic fluid."

"Yeah, but from *this* side, it looks like your father— presuming, of course, he was a Hawaiian prawn."

My wife and I had a post-OB-GYN-visit ritual. After every checkup we'd go to this little coffee shop across the street from the doctor's office and grab a bite to eat. I remember one of my wife's friends saying, "Boy, you are one great husband to go with your wife to every doctor's visit."

I said, "Well, I enjoy it, and I want to be there for her . . . Plus, the place across the street makes a banana muffin like you wouldn't believe."

Being out in public with an obviously pregnant woman has some strategic advantages. For one thing, there's nothing that makes strangers more hospitable. It's the VIP pass of all time.

"I'm sorry, we have no tables available."

"I see . . . Did you notice my wife's belly, by any chance?"

"Oh, look at that! You're pregnant! God bless you!

Right this way . . . Anthony, throw those deadbeats out of table seven. This lovely woman is pregnant."

People do anything for pregnant women. For many, it's the last vestige of social nicety. They may be rude and malicious toward every fellow man, but if a woman is bulging with child, most people, I was relieved to discover, will knock themselves out to be courteous. Seats are offered; groceries are carried. An occasional dessert is served on the house. Some couples, however, try to take advantage.

"Pardon me, I know this is not store policy, but my wife is expecting, so I'm wondering, could you give us a free pasta maker?"

At the same time, the indisputably pregnant belly also invites a lot of conversation and attention from people whose intimacy you don't necessarily welcome. It's such a *public statement.* When you see a pregnant woman out with her fella, you can deduce not only that she is with child, but also that *he's* the one who did it. "*That* guy did *that* to *that* woman." It's a pronouncement to the world that you've clearly been having sex. A pregnant belly is, essentially, a hickey for grown-ups.

And there was always the barrage of questions.

"Is this your first child?"

"Yes, it is."

"Boy or girl?"

"We don't know."

"When are you due?"

"Soon."

"How soon?"
"Soon."

It wasn't until they walked away that it hit me.
"Soon? The kid's coming soon?"
"Yeah, soon."
"Wow . . . I had no idea."

This Is It

I don't remember *everything*. I do recall we were eating pizza. My bride and I were eating really good pizza and watching a movie where Katharine Hepburn plays tennis. I remember that she played very well, and that it didn't seem to be a stunt double. That was definitely *her* hitting the ball. I remember Spencer Tracy was upset about something. And I remember my wife getting off the phone with the doctor and telling me, "He says we should get to the hospital *now*."

That's where my memory gets spotty.

I recall getting up to shut off the TV and cleaning up the kitchen remarkably thoroughly. I was wiping crumbs off the table, wrapping the unfinished pizza in Saran Wrap nice and tight, rinsing out glasses not once but two, three, even four times. I folded the pizza box in half, then in half again, and just before I got it down to the size of an overseas postage stamp, I heard my very pregnant wife say, "What are you doing?"

"What?"

"We have to *go.*"

"Oh, of course, I know . . . I was just cleaning up a bit."

I wasn't cleaning up just "a bit." I was scrubbing up with an attention to detail unprecedented in our years together. I had moved the couch so I could get a clear shot at vacuuming the *entire* carpet area.

"Maybe you could do that another time," my wife suggested violently.

Up to that evening, I had fully expected that with all the built-up tension and anticipation, I would virtually scoop my wife and child-to-be up in my arms and fly out the door the second I got the sign.

What I *didn't* expect—and didn't understand till months later—was that when the moment actually came, it would scare the hell out of me. I knew instinctively that the instant we stepped out of the house, our lives would never be the same. And I wasn't sure how much I wanted that. So my brain convinced me that if I slowed down and dragged everything out, I could postpone the next phase of my life. As it turns out, apparently you can't.

We got into the car, and I tried desperately to project an air of competence and authority.

"I'll drive," I said with great calm and magnanimity.

"Okay," she said.

Like *she* was actually thinking of driving.

I remember thinking that if ever I was legally allowed to drive too fast, it was now. Because even if we got stopped by a cop, I could say, "But, Officer, my wife's having a baby."

And then, if he did his part right, he'd push up the brim of his hat like cops did in the movies and say, "Well, why didn't you say so in the first place? Follow me!"

And then we'd get that really cool police escort, with sirens and everything.

I also remember it was really *quiet* in the car. All I heard was the thumping of my heart and that faint, grinding sound you sometimes hear when everything in the entire universe spins horribly out of control.

I looked over at my wife, who was holding her belly, her eyes closed. I squeezed her hand. She weakly attempted the beginning part of a smile, and then gave up.

I wanted to say something, but I didn't know what. I suspected that asking "You okay?" every eight seconds wasn't really helping.

When we stopped for a light, I looked at the guy next to us. I remember thinking how simple his life seemed. Wherever he was driving, I was willing to bet it didn't matter to him as much as our drive mattered to us.

I noticed his car. Then I'm pretty sure I said, "I was talking to Barry today, and they really love their Camry. They *did* go with the four-door."

My Beloved opened her eyes and turned her head ever so slightly toward me. Her pained expression told me to go with my first instinct.

"You okay?"

She nodded yes, and I drove us to the hospital.

The *main* difference between a hospital admission area and the Department of Motor Vehicles is that the DMV *really* doesn't care. Hospitals care, but they still make you fill out a clipboard-full of forms and "wait over there."

While the woman that I loved sat caressing the stomach that we *both* loved, I fumbled through my wallet, produced cards and IDs, and listed as many phone numbers and next of kins as my frazzled brain would offer up.

A steady stream of both green- and white-clothed hospital employees kept whizzing past us on their way to taking care of someone *not* us, and I remember feeling like immigrants must feel trying to get a cab from the airport.

"Will somebody just help us, *please?*"

Whenever anyone *did* talk to us, even if it was just to give us a map of fire exits and a pamphlet on the history of the hospital, I made a special effort to observe the name on their name tag and use it pointedly in a complete sentence.

"Thank you, *Dorothy*. We really appreciate that, *Dorothy*."

"How we doing on that room, *Darryl?* We'll be over

here, *Darryl*. Honey? *Darryl*'s going to check on the room for us."

I wanted to forge a bond with them not just because I thought it would make us stand out and get better service, but also because I was naive enough to think this was a special night for *them*, too, and that we would all correspond regularly for years to come.

"Hey, Dorothy, remember when Darryl tried to give an I.V. and he couldn't find a vein? That was something, huh?"

Of course, as soon as any of them took a coffee break and someone new came on duty, *they* became my new best friend.

"What is your name? Rosalinda? That's a very beautiful name . . . Listen, Rosalinda . . . I was wondering if you could help us . . ."

Once in a while I sucked up to people who didn't even work there. At one point I gave our whole medical history to a guy everyone kept calling "Doctor Cooper" only to find out he had a Ph.D. in art history and his wife happened to be in labor, too.

Eventually, someone led us to our room—a doctor or a nurse, or an unbelievably conscientious ice cream man. All I know is they were wearing white, and I was thrilled to see them.

And I remember lots of different people coming in with different stuff to do different things, the net result of which was that my wife was, in a matter of minutes, transformed from a Pregnant Woman into a Patient. Seeing

her in her little standard-issue hospital gown and wrist-
band, with her very own tan plastic pitcher of ice water
nearby, I got very sad. Up to this point, we had been
really lucky; since we'd been together, neither of us had
ever been in a hospital. But now, here she was, in a little
bed in the corner, with a button that you hit if you need
a doctor real fast. Just like sick people. And I could see it
was spooking her, too.

I sat on the edge of her bed and stroked her face.

"How you doing?"

I swear, there are only so many different ways you can
ask that question.

Her response surprised me.

"I want you to promise you'll remarry."

"Beg your pardon?"

"If anything ever happens to me, I want you to marry
someone and get on with your life."

"What are you talking about?"

"I mean, I don't want you to totally *forget* about me either. You know . . . you could be sad *periodically*, and
maybe you wouldn't necessarily take her to places that you
and I always went to, but I would want you to be happy."

"First of all—you're a big nut."

"I'm serious."

"You're going to be fine. Nothing's going to happen."

"It might. You don't know. What was that movie . . . ?"

"What movie?"

"The movie where the mother was giving birth and
they helped pull out the baby but the mother died?"

"*City Slickers*?"

"Yeah."

"Sweetie, that was a *cow*."

"Even so, remember? She thought everything was going to be fine, too, and then look what happened."

"Honey, that's so totally a different thing. First of all, the cow was living outdoors in bad weather for, like, thirty years. And second of all, it was a movie. And also keep in mind, that cow didn't have *me*."

That seemed to work. She smiled.

"I love you."

"Hey, what are you, kidding me?" I said. "I'm the one who loves *you*."

I don't remember any other day in my life where I went through every emotion there is. Inside of twenty-four hours, I felt joy, fear, love, anger, helplessness, wonder, and a numbness in my right hip from sitting funny on my wife's bed, which I know is not an emotion, but it's something I went through and why keep it a secret? There's a reason you can only go through all this at most every nine months. More often would be just unreasonable.

At some point, my wife's best friend came in. She had gone through this herself a couple of times and was someone my wife really wanted around. And while I had agreed to her being there, and was grateful for the support she provided, I have to admit it bugged me.

She's one of these women who speaks in really supportive tones, offering a nonstop stream of unconditional love that I really admire but can't help but make fun of.

"Isn't she doing great?" she asked me every thirty seconds.

"Boy, she sure is."

"You are doing so-ooooo great," she reiterated to my wife, clutching her hand tightly in her own.

"Yeah, sweetie, you really are," I threw in weakly from behind.

Now, I'm very well aware that if you ever plan on being totally selfless, the hour your wife gives birth to your child is as good a time as any to try. But I didn't like being dropped down to the Number Two position on the Support Team.

"Doesn't your wife look beautiful?" she said for my wife's ears but into *my* face. I'm thinking, "What does she think? I don't know how to say nice things myself? *I* know how to say nice things myself . . ."

Of course, what I *said* was, "Oh, wow, does she ever." I leaned over her to address my actual wife. "You really do, honey."

After a while, our most thoughtful of friends stepped out into the hall to give us some time together.

Alone again, with very little time to go, my bride and I looked at each other, and between her contractions and my feeble reminders to "Just breathe," we ran a last-minute search for girls' names.

"Sarah?"

"Nah . . . Stella?"

"It's a nice name if you're *Brando's* daughter . . . You sure I can't talk you into Aretha?"

"Oww owww owww . . ."

"Okay, just breathe . . ."

She breathed a few quick, sharp breaths and then I remembered something else.

"Oh, geez."

"What?"

"We forgot to get *values*."

"What?"

"Our child's going to be here any minute and we have no values."

At this point my wife contorted in pain, and then everything became a blur. There was a chunk of time—for the life of me, I couldn't tell you how long it lasted—where doctors came in, nurses scurried about, machines were wheeled around, mirrors were brought in . . . everybody was talking and moving and coaching and touching and prodding and sponging and gloving and crying and pulling and crowding—and through a haze of surreal commotion that veiled us somewhere entirely outside of place and time, I heard someone say, "Come here—you want to see?"

I actually said, "See *what*?"

"Your baby."

Oh. Right. I forgot that was happening today. I mean, I knew that's why we were there and everything, but . . .

I looked, and sure enough, something babylike was making its way into the world. No matter how many books you read, no matter how many tapes you watch, you still can't believe that this can happen. I looked up at my wife and was even more floored by what I saw next: the most radiant, beautiful woman I had ever imagined. In that moment—her hair curling with sweat across her forehead, crying and wincing in pain—in the midst of all that, was this exquisite and inescapably *feminine* being, doing exactly what she had to do, instinctively and splendidly. She was like an ad for Woman. Powerful and stunning. *That* I *do* remember.

It's a phenomenon beyond comprehension that women know how to do this. In order to give birth, it seems that God gives women a thousand times *more* stamina, resources, know-how, and smarts than they would have ordinarily. Ironically, for those very same hours, men get *less*. They get a little *less* intelligent, *less* resourceful, and *less* capable. And I don't think it's just coincidence. I choose to believe we become *less* of whatever we are specifically so that women can become *more* of whatever they are. It's a transfer. A gift of love. A shifting of the scales that helps perpetuate the cycle of Life, and then, later, when you get home, you can sort it all out and settle up.

The next thing I remember was the doctor looking up from his rolling front-row seat and gleefully pronouncing, "It's a boy!"

My heart took another in a now dizzying flurry of ecstatic jolts.

A boy! Yes!! I was thrilled not only because the mystery was over, but also because I could now openly confess to myself and to the world that, "Okay, I wasn't going to say anything, but I really *wanted* a boy!"

You're never allowed to admit that. Throughout pregnancy, you're only allowed to say, "We just want a healthy child." No one gets to say out loud that secretly, women want girls and men want boys. So you deny it. You convince yourself you genuinely have no preference.

But if it happens to work out your way, there's no way to pretend you're not smiling a teeny bit wider.

"Would you like to cut the cord?"

"What?"

The doctor handed me something frightening, shiny and metal, and said, "You're going to cut the cord, aren't you?"

Okay, here's the thing: I know everybody does it, and it's a magical moment and everything, but . . . what *is* that? Does merely being present at the birth automatically qualify a person to perform a medical procedure? If you visit your friend in the hospital, they don't invite you to take out the guy's appendix.

"Come on, go ahead . . . we'll be right here in case you screw it up . . ."

Of course, I did it. Because I wanted the experience of that magic moment, and, plus, I didn't want the doctor to think I was a wimp.

I had been forewarned that babies don't always look so pretty at birth, so I wasn't shocked by that. What did surprise me is that they come out with perfectly manicured fingernails. Neat, trim, little white lines around the whole front part—amazing. What do they need that for?

It's practically the only thing they have at birth that re-
sembles even remotely what it'll look like later on. And
there's nothing they have that could be less important.
Perhaps if they spent a little less time on their nails and
used it instead to, just for example, finish developing their
facial features, everyone would be better off. But, kids . . .
there's no talking to them.

For the next few minutes, doctors and nurses continued
to run around, they did a bunch of stuff, then they did
some *other* stuff, wrapped the baby up, and then placed
this brand-new person on his mother's chest.

I remember that my wife cried like a baby. The baby,
ironically, cried like an angry woman in her thirties. I
cried like a man exactly my age. The three of us cried,
and held each other, and cried a little more, and then
somebody nice must have packed us up and taken care of
everything, because somehow, sometime later, the three
of us—now and forever a family—went home.

Whose Idea Was This?

Walking into the house for the very first time with the child felt a bit like a honeymoon. The big difference, of course, is that when you carry a baby across a threshold, they're significantly lighter than the average adult bride, and also, we didn't immediately jump into a Jacuzzi and bad-mouth the band at the wedding.

Like the previous nine months, my wife did the actual carrying. I supervised.

"Careful, don't drop him . . . Honey, you almost dropped him there . . ."

The short journey from the front door to the baby's room took an inordinately long time, because though he weighed significantly less than a wheel of cheese, we choreographed the move like he was a piano.

"Okay . . . swing him around, now bring your end

over . . . watch out for the umbrella stand . . . you know what, let me move the sofa out of the way . . ."

Halfway to his room, I remembered.

"Oh, damn."

"What's the matter?"

"I forgot to get this on tape."

All that time during the pregnancy when I was supposed to be reading baby books and taking baby classes and learning baby CPR didn't go totally to waste because I did use the time to shop for the perfect *video camera*.

"Look, honey, this one has the screen that flips open, plus we can digitize the baby's face like they do on those cop shows."

Given all the time I put into getting the camera—not to mention all the time my wife put into making the baby—I thought it was well worth our while to make my wife repeat anything I failed to record for posterity.

"Hold it, I think I forgot to hit a button or something . . . Why can't I see his face?"

"Sweetie, I'd like to get the baby inside."

"Wait . . . how come . . . oh, okay. I had the lens cap on. Now, come in again."

"I'm not coming in again."

"Just go back a little bit."

"How far—the hospital?"

"No, just out the door. Can you make him wave?"

"He's a day old."

"I'm telling you, years from now, you'll thank me."

The thing they don't tell you in the video instruction manual is that babies don't make great subjects for moving pictures—what with them not *moving* a whole lot. And if you train your camera on the new mom, given what they feel is their less than sparkly appearance, you're likely to get their hand shoved into your lens, like a tobacco executive on *60 Minutes*. So you end up shooting the one member of the family who is willing to go before the camera—the dog.

"Here's *King* destroying a pair of knitted booties."

The arrival of children can be exhausting not only for people but also for *machines*. Our answering machine almost packed up and quit those first few days, because everyone you *know* calls, and never just once. We came home from the hospital, hit the button, and heard a mechanical voice on the verge of an emotional breakdown.

"You have one hundred and thirty-seven calls. The tape is now full . . . plus there's another nine I scribbled down by hand . . . and I know it's not my business, but there was a package at the door which I signed for because it said 'perishable.' " Which, you have to admit, for a little machine, is remarkably conscientious.

We, of course, saved the tape as a memento of the day. So years from now, our child can hear everyone who wished him well, along with a wrong number who kept calling looking for *Rita*.

Most of the messages from family and friends were addressed directly to the baby. Which is another one of those things that's too cute and yucky, and yet, invariably, something everyone does.

"Yes, this is a message for Baby *Schuyler* . . . welcome to town. And tell your parents Uncle Bisque and Aunt Cutlet called. They'll know who we are."

Or a popular variation—the "bypass-the-parents-and-bond-with-the-kid" calls.

"Tell your mommy and daddy that if they won't buy you a car when you get older, your Uncle Rudy'll take care of you . . ."

Some proud new parents will announce everything on the *outgoing* machine tape, so anyone who calls gets all the vital information.

"Please leave a message for Steve, Julie, and *Spartacus,* who was born Tuesday night, weighs seven pounds three ounces, is eighteen and a half inches tall, enjoys long baths and romantic walks in the woods, and currently smells like a combination of pineapple and potato gnocchi."

While this is certainly an *efficient* way of disseminating information, it doesn't make the caller feel particularly special. The implication is "If you've got access to a phone, you're all of equal importance to us. Telemarketers, wrong numbers, prowlers casing the house . . . everyone—come share our joy."

And share they did. No sooner did we transcribe all our familys' and friends' messages than we found ourselves inundated with the real thing.

.　.　.

A new child in the house is a huge tourist attraction. It's like Disneyland, except there the lines are longer and no one brings casseroles. Everybody has to come, everybody has to see.

And everybody has to *hold* the baby. I remember being naturally protective of our infant son. During those first few days, regulations were firmly established.

"Okay, you have to wash your hands before you handle the baby . . . You have to remove any sharp objects to be found on your person or clothing . . . If you've had a cold in the last eighteen months you must sit in the den until spring."

Even though we had only been parents for less than forty-eight hours, we felt perfectly justified in giving expert instructions to everyone. Like a newly founded country, we already had our laws, bylaws, and traditions.

"Um, Mom, that's not how he likes to be held . . . We always support his neck . . . like *this* . . ."

"Always?"

"Well, since yesterday."

Boy, nothing endears you to your parents more than telling them how to deal with babies.

"Do you remember me dropping you a lot when *you* were a baby?"

"Um, no, not really, but . . ."

"Did your *father* drop you a lot, that you recall?"

"No, but you don't . . ."

"So why don't you calm down and get your wife a sandwich?"

.   .   .

When everybody oohs and aahs over the baby, they're not just being nice; they're angling to see who the kid looks like. Up till then, I had no idea how explosive this issue is. I always assumed that everybody looks at least a little like one of their parents, and usually it changes. You may look like your father as an infant, but your mother as a toddler. What I didn't know is that when grandparents first hold their newborn grandchildren, family resemblance isn't just an interesting coincidence—it's a matter of utmost pride. Failure to look like the right side of the family is an insult and a dishonor.

When it was quite apparent to everyone that my son looked like his beautiful mother, my mother actually said to me, "So, you'll have another kid, *that* one'll look like us."

Everybody wants to talk to babies, but no one knows what to say. "Hello" is very popular. You can't *not* say it. You pick up a baby, you just start saying "Hello." Over and over. "Hello . . . hello . . . helllll-ooooo . . ." Like you're on the phone and the baby's just not picking up. In reality, they hear you fine—they're just waiting to hear what you say next.

Usually what comes next is a question. The inevitable high-pitched, dopey-voiced, grown-ups-talking-to-babies voice.

"Who's the cutest baby?"

"Who's got an itty-bitty nose?"

"Who's got a poopy diaper? You? Do you have a poopy diaper and an itty-bitty nose?"

First of all, these questions are way too easy. The reason babies don't answer is because they're insulted. They don't like being patronized.

"You *know* who the cutest baby is, so why ask? Give me a tough one."

"Who's that in the driveway? Is that Grandma pulling up in the driveway?"

But not *that* tough. That makes them angry.

"How the hell should I know who's in the driveway? I can barely see over this giant stuffed frog."

Plus, I think they resent questioning in general. It's like an interrogation.

"Who's that? What's that in your nose? Why are you crying? What did you do? And how do you explain your juice ending up on *his* bib?"

And they start sweating.

"Hey, I'm innocent, I tell ya. I've only been alive three and a half weeks . . . I just learned how to breathe, for crying out loud . . . I also, incidentally, just learned how to cry out loud . . ."

Observing my relatives with the baby, I realized they fall into a few different categories of adult-to-infant communication:

There's *The Greeter:*

"Who's that? That's your mommy. Who's that? That's your daddy . . ."

Who often works hand in hand with *The Tour Guide:*

"This is the living room, can you say living room? And

this is the foyer! You don't want to spill anything in the foyer . . ."

Who's not quite as annoying as *The Embarrasser:*

"Did you make a stinky? I think you made a stinky. I'm going to tell everyone you made a stinky, even though we're not a hundred percent sure . . ."

Or *The Entertainer:*

They just lean over the baby and make amusing noises.

"Ha-cha-cha—cha . . . Ha-cha-cha-cha . . . Boo-ta-boo-ta . . . chook-chook-chook-chook . . ."

These, of course, are all derivatives of the quintessential and official baby-speak noise—"Coochie coochie coo." I'm not sure how that became the industry standard, but it is. I imagine that at some point there must have been a meeting. "Coochie coochie coo" beat out perennial fa-vorite "goo-goo-gah-gah" and the straightforward but too-literal "Greetings, Small Bald Round One."

As we said our good-byes to friends and family, I noticed I anointed every male who attended this inaugural gath-ering with the title of "Uncle." Related or not, pretty much any male adult who spends more than ten minutes in the company of your child becomes an uncle.

"Uncle Mark was my college roommate . . . say good-bye to Uncle Mark . . ."

"Say hello to Uncle Cable Guy . . . Uncle Cable Guy was supposed to be here between eight and twelve . . ."

"Please don't stare at Uncle Car-Jacker. It makes him nervous."

Women, naturally enough, are automatically disqualified from being an Uncle. But the good news is that the qualifications for "Aunt" are just as negligible. Even if a friend comes over with a date that everyone *knows* he's never going to see again, you still say, "Say good-bye to Uncle Tommy and Aunt, uh, I'm sorry, what is it? *Barbie*. Right. Aunt *Barbie*."

Why are the requirements for these jobs so lax? And, more importantly, who wants more *relatives*?

After the last of the coffee was served and the hugs and kisses were distributed, the crowds did go home, and the exciting momentum that carried us through pregnancy, and then through all the drama and elation of the birth, started to subside. In its place, staring us in the face, was a vast unknown called "The Rest of Our Lives."

We went upstairs, took the baby to the room we had set up, stocked, and decorated to within an inch of its life, looked at him, then at each other, and realized, "Now what?"

We had no idea how one starts the process of actually *being* parents.

The first impulse is to fall into "host" mode.

"Would you like a drink or something? Diet Coke? A beer? Oh, no, of course . . . I forgot—your people don't drink . . . You want to freshen up? There's a bathroom down the hall—Oh, your people do it right in their pants, don't you? . . . You want to watch TV? Video? I got the *Godfather* trilogy . . . Tell you what, we're going to probably eat in an hour or so . . . so why don't you just, uh . . . sit there, and we'll watch you. Okay? Okay."

Just a Few Things to Worry About

When you first have your baby home, your brain is seized with a plethora of potential dangers.

"I could drop him. I could drop something on him. I could roll on top of him in my sleep . . ."

These are big fears you can instantly envision. But there are plenty of ways you can harm a baby that you don't even see coming.

I'm changing my son's pajamas, and he starts screaming. I panic. "What? What could it be? I've done everything right. I'm blocking him so he can't roll off, I cleared away everything in a two-mile radius that he could pull down on top of him, I dimmed the light so as to not damage his little retinas, I put on soothing music for his listening and dancing pleasure . . ."

I even did the little thing where you gather up the sleeve at the cuff, so you can pull him through in one shot, as opposed to the go-in-the-sleeve-with-him and snake his arm through inch by inch, like a little arthroscopic camera. So why's he screaming at me?

Apparently, when you pull a baby's fist through a sleeve, some of his fingers don't always make it. Halfway through the process, a pinky can jump out into the middle of the road. So while you're singing a catchy melody from *Peter Pan* to his face, you're quietly breaking off a good one-fifth of his favorite hand. You can't see that coming.

Simple things like clothes can be riddled with danger. Did you know that their feet can get caught in your shirt pocket? Pockets that have been unopened since you bought the shirt become a treacherous baby-foot magnet.

Did you know that when you pull a T-shirt over a kid's head, the entire head can get stuck in the head hole, and they seem to have no idea that it will be over in one thirty-secondth of an inch? They become engulfed in fear, believing they're stuck in an endless black void of time and space. Maybe they're reliving the trauma of birth. Who knows? I suppose *we* wouldn't like that either. If every time our pants were too tight, we thought we were getting sucked into the center of the earth, we might be a little more careful getting dressed, too.

But there are so many things that can go wrong, it's unbelievable. In the name of preparation, I made up a brief list:

You could hold him too tight.
You could hold him too loose.

You could carry him up the stairs and trip on your pants.

You could trip on *nothing*—just the sheer pressure of hoping to God you don't trip.

You could toss him up just when the phone rings and answer it instead of catching him.

You could toss the baby in the air just as a stork is flying by, which snags your baby midair and delivers him to another family.

You could make him *wave* to someone who doesn't wave back, and he's so traumatized he's never able to hail a cab.

You could park his carriage near a building that, unbeknownst to you, is targeted by left-wing terrorists.

You could diaper him so tight you cut off his circulation.

You could try to call your pediatrician and mistakenly call your podiatrist, who tells you the best thing for your baby's cold is Dr. Scholl's foot powder, which ironically cures the cold but leaves the baby smelling forever like a very old tennis shoe.

You could be so sleep deprived that you accidentally feed a cold and starve a fever. Or is it spring forward and fall back? Whatever it is, you do something bad.

You could carry him outside in the "football hold" for so long you think you're in a game and accidentally punt.

You could wind the mobile over his crib so tight that the whole crib takes off like a helicopter and flies through the roof.

You could absentmindedly fold up the stroller with the kid still *in* it, and not discover the mistake till days later when you're setting up for another stroll.

You could take him to the beach and he gets too much sun.

You could be so afraid of him getting too much sun that you bring the child out only at night and he becomes a vampire.

You could put him in diapers that have such extra-strength, super-duper sticky tabs that he inadvertently drags home your neighbor's dresser.

You could *beep* his belly button with a finger that has a hangnail and puncture him.

You could baby-proof the house so thoroughly that no one can get out.

You could accidentally touch his schmeckle in such a way that thirty years from now he writes a book which shames you throughout the nation.

You could feed him a bottle that's too hot.

You could feed him a bottle that's too *cold*.

You could feed him a bottle that's *just right* but actually belongs to three angry bears.

You could be so groggy that instead of milk you grab the dog's stomach medicine, put it in the baby's bottle, and the next morning they're both licking their own bellies.

You could forget to take off the safety cap under the bottle nipple, causing the baby to suck so much air he starts hyperventilating so you try to help by putting a paper bag over his head, which is when your

wife walks in and rightfully takes the child away and
he has to grow up without a father.

You could burp him so hard he needs a chiropractor.

You could give him a bath and the water's too hot.

You could give him a bath and the water's too *cold*.

You could make the water just right, but the same
damn bears come in and rip the place up.

You could put the baby too low in the plastic bathtub
so he kicks open the plug and gets sucked down the
drain.

He could get sucked only *halfway* down the drain and
you can't figure out which way to pull him out.

You could bathe him and get soap in his eyes.

You could bathe him and get soap in *your* eyes, you
can't see what you're doing and end up poking *him*
in the eye anyway.

You could use "No Tears" shampoo so it doesn't matter if it gets in his eyes—only it's past the expiration
date, so tears come.

You could leave him in the water so long he becomes
permanently wrinkled and people think he's a shar-
pei puppy.

You could actually throw out the baby with the bath-
water.

You could clip his nails and a nail piece flies off the
clipper and up his nose.

You could drop a pacifier, it lands rubber side down
on a tile floor, bounces into his ear, and for the rest
of his life people can only talk to him on one side.

You could have a magnet on the refrigerator in the

shape of a little hamburger, which he eats and, though it doesn't hurt him, twenty years later he gets lost on a camping trip because his compass keeps pointing to his stomach.

You could be taking cute, naked-butt baby pictures, reposition him one too many times, and he ends up in the emergency room with rug burns.

You could get him looking so cute in those baby-butt pictures that the people at Michelin use him for an ad, and while shooting the ad, a tire rolls over his legs.

You could step on a rake and the handle flies up and hits you in the face like a Laurel and Hardy movie and the kid laughs so hard, he hurts himself.

You could pat him on the head and your wedding band hits him in the soft part of his skull and scrambles his brain.

His mother could be in another room and call for some scissors and without thinking you hand them to him and say, "Hurry, run!"

You could be holding the baby while talking on the cordless phone, and when you hang up, you put them *both* down and for days you can't find either one of them.

You could affectionately rub his head after walking across a thick carpet and the static electricity makes his diaper catch on fire . . .

Any of these things *could* happen.
But fortunately I'm not, by nature, a worrier.

Translating Your Child

Those first few nights, every time our baby cried, we sprinted to his side. Because every cry sounded like an emergency.

"What's the matter, Pumpkin? Are you hungry? Thirsty? Still upset about losing that umbilical cord?"

But all he'd say was, "WWAAAAAHHHHH."

What we didn't understand is that babies have a veritable library of cries, varying in pitch, duration, and emotional intensity—and it's your job to figure them out.

"Waaaaaaahhhhh-gk!"

"Is that 'hungry'?"

"No, 'hungry' is higher pitched and a little more nasal."

"Waaaaaaahhhhh-gk!"

"Diaper?"

"Could be, hard to say."

The differences are very subtle. For example, our son's "The-light-is-coming-in-from-outside-and-scaring-me" cry is almost identical to his "The-drool-on-my-sheet-is-hardening-and-cutting-me-across-the-cheek" cry. And his "Something-you-ate-had-pepper-in-it-and-I'm-very-resentful" cry is only one little throaty nuance away from "Remember that German shepherd the other day? I hate him."

In time, you become an expert at not only interpreting your child's cries and sounds, but all his quirks, likes, and dislikes.

"Oh, you better take that orange shirt off him . . . orange, for some reason, makes him hiccup."

A lot of times, you can get carried away with this new skill. My wife convinced herself early on that our son had remarkably specific musical tastes, and she could break it down for you by song and artist.

"He loves the Beatles . . . John a little more than Paul, and really responds strongly to George. Loves 'Taxman,' can't make it through 'Let It Be.' "

All new parents pride themselves on being able to interpret their children because not only are we showing off our own laser-keen parenting know-how, but we also get to ascribe to our children abilities and intellect that truthfully they don't really have.

When my son started saying "Da-da," I—as might be expected—was convinced that he was not only singularly gifted but was in constant conversation specifically with *me*.

I began to show off our little performance piece to anyone who would listen.

"Watch this . . . Okay, Son, what's my name?"

"Da-da."

"Huh? What'd I tell you . . . Okay, who's married to Ma-ma?"

"Da-da."

"You see how smart he is? He knows lots of other stuff, too. Watch . . . Okay, what was the name of the movement in modern art that was popularized in Europe in the early nineteen-twenties?"

"Da-da."

"Da-da-ism, that's entirely correct."

It's Your Turn

People often ask me, "What's the difference between couplehood and babyhood?"

In a word? Moisture.

Everything in my life is now more moist.

Between your spittle, your diapers, your spit-up and drool, you got your baby food, your wipes, your formula, your leaky bottles, sweaty baby backs, and numerous other untraceable sources—all creating an ever-present moistness in my life, which heretofore was mainly dry.

Certainly, there have been other changes in my life since the arrival of my child: I feel an even greater commitment to my wife and our marriage. I feel an instinctive, primal love of which I did not know I was capable. I feel a heightened sense of responsibility toward my community and planet Earth.

But above all, it's the moisture. It's just really moist now.

Before we go any further, allow me to take a moment to clarify the various *categories* of moisture. There's *spit,* which is the wet stuff that's in your baby's mouth; *spittle*— spit that's *left* the mouth and is hanging off your baby's face in long, suspended, pendulous gobs; and *drool,* which is secreted during sleep and collects in large, lukewarm pools.

And, last but certainly not least, *spit-up* (often referred to by the slang *"cheese"*), which is hot, lumpy, and frankly too repulsive to discuss any further. "Cheese" has an al- most magnetic attraction to adult clothing, and the more expensive the garment or the more pressing your need to get out of the house, the more likely the chance this sub- stance will be propelled out of your baby and onto your freshly dry-cleaned attire. Cheese just loves this.

One of the wonderful aspects of these various emissions is that they serve to bond and unite all new parents. I can now spot new parents on the street—even without their kids. Just look for a three-by-four-inch damp patch on their shirts between their shoulders and ribs, the part where very recently a youngster's head was resting and emitted a steady flow of sweet, sticky babyness. They leave a trail—not unlike snails. And this trail becomes an emblem, a team logo, a crest to be worn with pride. And a towel.

·   ·   ·

Way before your kid even gets here, everyone in sight does their level best to scare you about diapers.

"Oh, I can't wait to see *you* handling diapers . . . Hey, everybody—can you imagine *him* changing diapers? . . . Getting up in the middle of the night to change those diapers . . . you'll see . . . I mean, have you ever actually changed a diaper? . . . Boy, you're not going to like changing diapers . . ."

Okay, first of all, let me say this: *Thank God* for diapers. Because the alternative is unthinkable. Would you want to live in a world where there were *no* diapers? A world where the very items intended to be accumulated by diapers were *not* accumulating but rather flying through the air undeterred? I, for one, would not.

Second of all, let's get a grip here; it's not that big a deal. Especially in the beginning. I understand that once you hit the two-year-old point, diapering is pretty much like changing pants on a hobo. But on a newborn, it's almost a pleasure.

Admittedly, the actual skill takes a few practice rounds. The first time I tried to put a new diaper on my baby, I yanked the little Velcro strap too jerkily and actually punched the little guy in the jaw. A real solid shot, too. I knew instinctively that this could not be correct. Unless you're specifically trying to raise a welterweight, continual deliverance of powerful uppercuts is not advised when handling newborns.

And, of course, we had the Great Diaper Debate— cloth versus disposable. We wanted to be environmentally sensitive, considering that the accumulation of disposable diapers is now engulfing a good one-third of the world's landmass. In descending order of size, I believe it's now Asia, North America, and then Huggies.

So we vowed to eschew the convenience of these Earth-chokers and instead use only recyclable cloth diapers, nobly shouldering the added responsibility of constant laundering and increased waste-product handling. This lasted literally an *hour*. The first time you handle a particularly offensive diaper, you want it out of your hands and out of your house so fast that you're more than glad to look the other way and let someone else's parents save the planet.

Some people—and it's usually older people—are still genuinely amused by the idea of *men* changing diapers. It's hard to remember that not too long ago, fathers weren't big diaperers. As we approach the millennium, however, no guy—unless he's been cryogenically frozen since 1957—can possibly get away with *not* changing diapers.

Having said that, the instinct within men to throw the job over to women is alive and well. One night, we were sitting around the house with some friends, enjoying a Sunday afternoon, His Royal Infantness playing happily on the floor nearby.

Suddenly, a powerful aroma, not unlike that of a construction site Porta Potti, permeated the room. And *someone* had to change it.

In theory, I wouldn't presume for a second that it necessarily would be my wife's responsibility, but nonetheless, I turned to my wife and said, "Honey . . . ?," the implication unmistakably being, "Take care of that, would you?"

My wife, interestingly enough, was giving me the very same look.

And it is here that you learn the three words that become the chief verbal staple of any household with a baby: *It's Your Turn.*

This phrase is the theme song of any marriage once it goes from Two to Three.

"I just changed him twenty minutes ago . . . It's your turn."

"I've been watching him all day. It's your turn!"

"I simply cannot stand up; it's your turn!"

This all-purpose phrase also works as a marital *greeting.* The "Hi-sweetie-how-was-your-day" of yesteryear is now replaced with the more simple, direct, and mildly irritated "It's *your* turn."

Before you have a child, you and your spouse are many things to each other: friends, lovers, competitors, partners . . . Upon producing a child, you relate to each other primarily as *sentries.*

The two of you are guards who rotate shifts monitoring and protecting your new charge.

When Baby enters your world, there's no time for intimate conversation between Husband and Wife. In fact,

the extent of conversation often consists solely of the re-
porting of Baby's "eating-sleeping-pooping" status—just
before the changing of the guard.

"Hi."

"He ate, he napped, he needs to be changed."

"I just walked in. Can I take a shower?"

"You should've showered before we had a kid. *It's your
turn.*"

Then, like buck privates relieving one another at
Guantanamo, you're on duty and your wife gets a four-
hour pass.

When it comes to knowing *when* to change your child,
there are *four essential tools*: smelling, looking, squeezing,
and peeking.

It usually begins with the smell—a kind of "silent
alarm" that lets you know it's time for a fresh diaper.

In an attempt to keep the "hands on" part of the diapering experience to an absolute minimum, you next
eyeball the diaper. Is it drooping? Perhaps swaying a bit?
Does the child look like he's been riding a horse for many
days? If so, it may be changing time.

But sometimes looks can be deceiving. So, for further
confirmation, you unceremoniously lift your child up and
sniff him like a cantaloupe.

"*Sniff, sniff . . .* he either needs to be changed or won't
be ready to serve for three or four days."

Then you've got your *squeezers*, the parents who take
the melon analogy to the extreme, and frankly should take
a good hard look at themselves.

And for the final test—you *peek*. No niceties, no subtlety, you just pick up the child, pull back his pants, and look inside.

If you're right, and the child needs changing, you're vindicated.

If he *doesn't* need changing, you both feel a bit foolish. You, for being so off the mark and harassing a perfectly innocent child, and the child, of course, because someone's pulling back their pants and looking in. Usually the baby will turn back to you as if to say, "May I help you?" And your honest answer is, "No, thanks, we're just looking."

The only good thing to come out of this embarrassing standoff is that for a fleeting moment, you get a freebie look at a cute naked baby bottom. And it's never a disappointing visual. Especially in this circumstance, where you're looking from above and can see only the top half—the net result of which looks like a miniature Ten Commandments.

It should be noted, also, that changing diapers is not without its *entertainment value*.

When you're changing a diaper, one of the things you have to do is *lift* the baby's little legs, bend them, and swivel them. Sort of like when you're cooking a chicken and you look underneath to see how the potatoes are doing.

Now, sometimes, if you swivel a little too far, a special little gust of wind will whiz by your knuckles. An appreciative, resonant "Ode to Lunch." What I discovered is that if, at this time, you continue to bend their knees and rotate them from the waist down, you can alter not only the *tone* but the *duration* of the sound. It's not unlike the mechanics of a bagpipe—though without the woolen kilt and sense of celebration. But musical nonetheless.

With the proper technique, you can get them to sing entire tunes. Well, not "sing" exactly, but I did extract from my son's bottom the first few bars of "Nearer My God to Thee," and, if I'm not mistaken, a lovely medley from *Carousel.*

And this is a newborn—imagine if he took a lesson.

And one more thing (and I swear this is the last thing I'm going to say about poop). Sometimes when you're changing the baby, you may notice that there is a—and I'm really not trying to be rude—but sometimes you notice a big stain in the middle of the baby's back. Not a *continuous* stain, mind you. Not a trail from the diaper all the way up his pajamas, but rather a little special area in the middle, stretched out in the shape of Cuba. Above it and below, it's totally clean.

So first of all, I have to ask—how do you poop *up*? It's not like the baby was swinging upside down. He wasn't hanging by his feet from a trapeze and the roar of the crowd made him lose it. He was sitting down, like a regular person, and this stuff flew up.

But even more mystifying to me, how did it *skip* the area leading up to the spot? Right before Cuba, it's clean and laundered. The little Gulf of Mexico area is unscathed. It's a phenomenon.

My theory—because I *have* given this thought—is that this particular skill may be a remnant of prehistoric times that slowly, as we've evolved, became obsolete. Something we no longer needed—like the Tail. Maybe thousands of years ago it was important. To a lizard. It's possible that to a lizard, pooping straight up was not only vital to survival, but perhaps even a sign of impressive upbringing. Picture two lizards at the sink in the ladies' room.

"And this guy I just met, he is *so cool*. Really great skin, totally scaly, and *long*. And get this: He can poop 140 feet straight up. Standing on the ground, he can actually hit a pterodactyl in the throat."

"What a dreamboat . . ."

The Big
Tired Elephant

When you're the parents of a new child, all the craving and desire you've ever felt for sex is transferred over to *sleep*. It's like somebody sneaked into your brain, found the wires going to the sex button and the sleep button, and just switched them.

I didn't realize how extensive the change was till I found myself one day staring at a lingerie ad with a photo of a beautiful, seductive, young woman sprawled practically naked across a satin-sheeted bed, and all I could think was, "Man, that bed looks comfortable."

I've Never Been This Tired, Ever

No question about it, sleep deprivation is the worst thing about being a new parent. Period, end of discussion. Given the choice, I would gladly diaper my kid into his late twenties if for those same years you promised me a solid eight hours a night.

Being sleep deprived (or the politically correct "consciousness challenged") is like undergoing a medical experiment. One by one, you watch your mental faculties slip away.

The first to go is language. Sometime during those forty-five minutes between feedings when you actually are asleep, a little man comes and takes your *nouns* away.

"Honey, when you go to the uh . . . ."

"To the what?"

"To the . . . whad'ya call it . . . the place? With the things . . . they have things that you can buy . . . ."

"The store?"

"Yes, thank you. To the store . . . Make sure we pick up some . . . some, uh . . ."

"What?"

"Little . . . um . . ."

"What do you want?"

"You know. They're small, you stick them in the ears . . ."

"Earrings?"

"No. Fuzzy things."

"Q-Tips?"

"Yes, exactly. Q-Tips."

This, of course, presumes you have the strength to get that much of a sentence out. During our child's first few months, my wife and I both thought we were going *deaf.* We literally could not hear half of every sentence spoken. It turns out we were just out of steam, too weak to speak audibly.

"I spoke to fhmwlmmn . . ."

"What?"

"Yesterday. I spoke to fhmlawhlawhmn . . ."

"Okay, stop right there, look me in the face and say that again slowly."

"I SPOKE TO THE PHARMACIST. THE PHAR-MACIST. What's the MATTER with you?"

Which brings us to the next unfortunate deterioration. You're reduced to mankind's most elemental mode of survival—*crankiness.* Just when you need each other most, you're snapping at each other like sarcastic little turtles.

"Is this *your* underwear?"

"No, it's Margaret Thatcher's. And I can't tell you why I have it."

Ugly rivalries break out like wildfire. When the baby wakes up in the middle of the night, for example, one of you has to get up and deal with it. And each of you will do anything *not* to be that one.

The game goes like this:

The baby starts crying. You both pretend you're asleep and don't hear a thing. But the baby is *crying;* he needs to see somebody. So, while still pretending to be asleep, you "accidentally" poke your elbow into your loved one's ribs. If that fails to prod them awake, you nonchalantly roll over and slam into them, making a few fake snoring noises to show how asleep you are.

Not to be outdone, your partner then rolls into *you,* throwing a hand in your face while "stretching." The person who knocks the other person out of bed first wins. However, never under any circumstances ask, "You awake?" Because then all your partner has to do is lie there, and *they* win.

As the volume of your child's cries intensifies, you both feel progressively more guilty lying in bed—even though only seconds have actually elapsed. So Round Two begins, in which you both give up the charade of being asleep and instead compete over who's got the best excuse *not* to get up.

"Would you get up and see why he's crying? I've got a big meeting tomorrow morning."

"So do I."

"Yes, but is *your* meeting at the *Kremlin?* . . . I didn't think so."

Just because a baby cries, I discovered, doesn't mean there's always something wrong. Sometimes babies wake up for no real reason. They just want to check if they're doing it right.

"This is Sleeping, right?"

"Exactly."

"I just lie here?"

"That's right."

"Okay."

Then back to sleep they go.

And then there's the very specific condition that only babies get called "overtired," where they're too tired— and frankly, too stupid—to just sleep.

"Why's he crying?"

"He's tired."

"Why doesn't he go to sleep?"

"He's too tired. He's *over*-tired."

"Too tired to sleep?"

"Yes."

"So why don't *I* go to sleep, and he can watch *me* for a while?"

See, grown-ups don't have this problem. If I'm tired, just give me a chair and a room where people aren't specifically shouting, and I will fall asleep. It doesn't take a lot of experience or dexterity to do this. It's not like "hungry," where babies sadly lack the means to feed themselves. Sleeping is simple. Just shut your eyes and see what happens. But babies have not yet figured out that Sleep is the antidote to Tired.

For many new parents, a Sleeping Baby becomes all they ask out of life.

"Please go to sleep . . . I beg you to go to sleep . . . everybody shut up, so he can go to sleep . . . Okay, he just *fell* asleep . . . hurry up and pat him so he *stays* asleep . . . Now if anyone wakes my baby up, I will shoot them."

You get nuts. I started barking at people in public places. Restaurants, malls, stadiums—places where it's one's God-given right to converse—I've actually gone over to strangers and "shushed" them.

"I *see* you're having a party, but couldn't you all sing 'Happy Birthday' to your mom in the parking lot? My kid is trying to sleep—shhhh!!!"

I became the world's librarian.

The most popular piece of advice we got from our friends was, "When your baby sleeps, you better sleep, too. It's your only chance."

The *second* most popular piece of advice was, "When your baby sleeps, you better hurry up and do everything you want to do, because when they're up, you won't have a chance."

So, according to the experts, when your baby sleeps, you have to go to sleep, while simultaneously doing everything you couldn't do when the baby was awake.

Any way you figure it, those precious windows of opportunity between "He's cranky because he wants to sleep" and "He's cranky because he just woke up" are to be treasured. And maximizing this Golden Time requires precision planning.

"Okay, if we feed him now, he should be asleep in the car. Maybe we can have a conversation. If we take him out of the car just right, he'll very likely sleep through soup, salad, and possibly the main course. He'll definitely be stirring by coffee. Flip him over quick, that'll knock him out for dessert."

Getting your child to sleep becomes such a blinding obsession, I myself would often lose sight of the big picture: What is the actual goal here? *Constant* sleep? *No* awake-time? *Zero* consciousness?

I mean, we must accept that at *some* point babies have to be awake. They didn't come to the planet just to sleep. Are we determined to get them asleep just so we can get a taste of what life was like *before* we had kids?

Because if we are, then tell me again—why did we have a kid? Just to lie there and look soft and fuzzy? We could have just gotten, say, a peach. A Saint Bernard. A narcoleptic houseguest. Or why not just get a huge chenille bathrobe? Chenille bathrobes are fuzzy and just lie there—why don't we just get us one of those and name it *Michael*? And the great thing about a bathrobe is, no matter how hard you slam a door, it ain't getting up.

The Mad Patter

I used to think that patting babies on the back was simply to "burp" them: to coax little gas bubbles out of their tiny digestive systems. But, oh, it is so much more.

First and foremost, it is primarily a tool of Distraction. Anytime you see them on the brink of waking up or crying, or detect even the slightest hint of displeasure, start patting. Essentially, you want to talk them out of it. They can be ready to absolutely bawl and explode into a dissertation on "Why Everything Sucks," but if you pat them just right, they'll stop and turn to you, slightly confused, as if you bumped into them in a crowded airport.

"Hmm? Beg your pardon? . . . Somebody say something? . . ."

Then they spend the next few moments trying to isolate the patting. "Where's that damn rattling coming from? . . . Anybody else feel a shaking? Like a 'thump,

thump, thump, thump?' . . . Nobody? Okay, maybe it's just me . . . as I was about to say . . . Waaahhh . . .'' And then they go ahead and cry anyway. But for a second there, you feel very clever. You momentarily outwitted an infant.

If you keep it going long enough, you sort of retune their entire body frequency to the rhythm of your patting. They will ultimately surrender, and go for a ride on your little percussive train.

Sometimes, I must admit, I get carried away. Because patting out the same, rhythmic thump can get a bit monotonous. So you find ways to amuse yourself. You add a few syncopations. You double up the beat, change the feel, transition into a little waltz time, jazz it up, thump out the opening drumbeat of the ''Sergeant Pepper'' reprise—whatever your mood dictates. But you can become mesmerized by your own thumping prowess. One time I had the baby in my arms, didn't realize I had already successfully patted him to sleep, and for another thirty minutes banged out an entire Tito Puente album on his spine.

Nobody wants to see a baby cry. But the truth of the matter is that, sometimes, *on their way* to crying, babies *warm up* for a cry, and it can be pretty damn cute.

Usually, when they just wake up, babies feel obligated to cry about *something*, even if they're not sure what. So they scan their little brains, thinking of a viable source of discontent. Plus, they don't have quite the *energy* one needs to cry, so they just start to squint their eyes and lower the corners of their mouth, until the entire mouth becomes a downward-facing curve. Like the sales chart of a company about to go under. Or the "Tragedy" half of the Comedy/Tragedy masks.

The challenge I set for myself is, How long can I let that drama-award face go before allowing actual tears? How close to the edge of hysterical can I let him get? What you want to do is catch him just a microsecond before he spills over into a wail. Timing is crucial: If you wait too long, you leave the category of "Fun-Loving Parent" and enter the world of "Cruel for No Damn Reason." It's a game of risk, the parental version of bungee jumping.

There are those who would belittle my expertise in the art of Baby Patting, and argue that thumping someone's torso continuously is not that difficult. If I weren't around, they maintain, the job could easily be performed by a metronome with an oven mitt. But they underestimate what I have accomplished. I've become more than a mere *tapper*, more than a pedestrian *thumper*. I've become, in essence, a great *hypnotist*. The Amazing Daderino.

"Give me a baby on the brink, I will do the rest."

Even if they're totally awake, I can put them down.

"Look into my eyes . . . Are you looking? . . . Just a moment . . . wait a minute . . . and . . . *Voilà*—ladies and gentlemen, I give you: a Sleeping Baby."

It used to be, if you put people to sleep, you were considered Dull; now, it's a Gift.

.   .   .

Once your child is asleep, however, if you're not careful transferring him out of your arms, you'll wake him up. Then you have to start your act all over again.

Many is the time I've patted my son to sleep on my chest, and then, too scared to wake him, I elect to just lie there. Whatever I had planned to do I forgo and prostrate myself with a small human being clinging to my neck, doing my best to remain perfectly inert. Like Sean Connery and the tarantula in *Dr. No.* (Although with a tarantula, you get bitten and it's over. With a baby, if they start crying, your whole afternoon is shot.)

Not that lying with a sleeping baby on your chest is the worst thing in the world, either. In fact, it's one of the sweetest pleasures I've ever tasted. An entire person curled up between your collar bone and stomach, covering and warming your heart, all the while breathing little bursts of perfect air onto your neck. It's not hard to imagine why moms love the sensation of breast-feeding. For dads, breast-*napping* is about as close as we get.

While you hold your sleeping child, you envision all the wonderful things you hope to do, and all the details of the charmed life you have planned together.

And then they wake up and have no idea who you are. Babies awaken slightly disoriented, with a look that's half Angel and half Lost Tourist. They look up at you like you're vaguely familiar, but they can't quite place the face.

"And you are . . . ?"

"I'm Dad."

"No, that's not it . . ."

"It's me. Your daddy."

"Were you here earlier?"

"Of course, don't you remember? I tapped you to sleep . . . Half an hour ago . . . ? Tall guy . . . ? Married to Mom . . ."

It starts to ring a bell.

"Mom . . ."

"The one with the milk."

"Oh, yes, of course, of course . . . Dad! How are you?"

Step Aside, Please

Given how much more naturally competent my wife is at almost all areas of parenting, if I do discover an area where I may have a leg up, I jump on it. I pounce on it like a lion on meat.

One day I walked by to see my wife changing our son's diaper, and I witnessed what, for my money, was a rather perfunctory once-around of the boy's young privates. I said, "Babe, what are you doing?"

She was thrown.

"Why?"

I stepped in with unwavering authority.

"That is *not* how we wash balls."

"Is that right?"

"That's right."

"Sweetie, I've been changing diapers pretty consistently for a while now, and . . ."

"Maybe. But let me ask you something."

"What."

"D'ya *have* balls yourself?"

"No, but . . ."

"All right, then."

"So what? That doesn't mean that—"

"Well, I think I know a *lit-tle* bit more about the subject than you do. So . . . do you mind?"

"Fine."

And as she stepped away, I took over.

"Thank you."

When she was out of the room, I looked down at my son, who I'm pretty sure was smiling at me appreciatively, and I *winked* at him. It was the first time I'm aware of having a specifically *male bonding moment* with my son. (And certainly the first time I ever winked at anybody.)

"Don't worry, Daddy's here. Daddy knows what you need . . ."

As I proceeded to diaper him, I took the opportunity to wax philosophical about all things masculine and intimate.

"You know, Son . . . as you grow older and bigger and stronger, this area will be very important to you. Oh, I know it means nothing to you *now*. Now it's just the area that gets wetter than every place else. But you mark my words: This area will be your friend."

Powder, powder, sprinkle, sprinkle.

"But it's also important that it not be your *only* friend. I don't want this area to rule your life as it does with so many fine young men. So much energy in life is spent comparing and competing and discussing this area, but you must remember that this is not the true measure of a man. You know, years ago . . ."

And then I noticed he was staring at me. This whole time, he'd been looking at *me* looking at *him*. I could hear the therapy bills ringing up.

"And that's why, Doctor, to this day I cannot put on a bathing suit if there is a man talking."

Quickly, I turned my gaze elsewhere and finished diapering him without looking. It was at this point that my bride walked back in the room.

"Sweetie . . ."

"What?"

"You're diapering his *thigh*."

"Huh? Oh, I know . . . hey, why don't you take over? You know what you're doing."

Is That a Needle in Your Hand, or Are You Just Glad to See Me?

Taking your child for his first checkup is a big milestone. But it's a mixed bag. On one hand, it's exciting, because your baby, who was born seemingly minutes ago, is already mature enough to be doing things as mundane as having a doctor's appointment. He's like a person. With things to do.

"I've got to stop at the dry cleaner's, then I've got a doctor's appointment, and then I've got a three o'clock reading of *Here Comes a Fire Truck*. So let me pencil you in for tomorrow."

Clearly time is flying, progress is being made.

On the other hand, your baby is in a doctor's office. He's certainly not going to enjoy it. It's bright, loud, and smells like a hospital, a place he didn't particularly enjoy the first time. So it's hard to imagine anything good coming out of this. All you hope for is that you get a perfect bill of health, which means, best-case scenario, you leave with the exact same baby you walked in with. While you wait in an examining room for the doctor to finish prodding and poking someone else's baby, you sit and memorize the posters of disgusting ear infections and faulty lung scenarios that you hadn't managed to worry about yet, but are certainly happy to add to the list *now*. So, even if everything goes great, *you* personally still leave a little worse off for the wear.

When the doctor finally comes in, they immediately—if they're smart—say how beautiful your baby is, how much he's grown, etc. This is, frankly, all you want to hear.

Then you hand the baby over to be examined—a moment that feels somehow a little *biblical*. Gingerly and fearfully, you make of your firstborn a sacrificial offering to a Being with abilities far beyond your own. You have nothing but your faith. And the hope that those diplomas hanging on the wall are not forged.

It's kind of like bringing your car into the shop.

"Uh, yeah, it's not making the noise now, but I definitely heard it yesterday, so, you know, why don't you just poke around and tell me what you think, because I myself know virtually nothing."

And I felt sad because I realized my son was about to take his first Test. He might not have known it, and he might not have studied for it or worried about it, but the fact that he was—consciously or unconsciously—about to respond, or fail to respond, correctly or incorrectly, and have points added or subtracted from his record—it all just broke my heart.

Ultimately, you realize you can't help him, so you merely wish him good luck and tell him to "do the best you can."

But nothing prepared me for the real heartbreak—the moment of The Shot. The actual injection. You know your baby has to get these shots, but that moment of pain and the look of betrayal in his eyes still haunt me. Babies have no idea there's a shot coming. They don't see the nurse shooting an arc of fluid out of the needle. And if they did, they'd probably think it's just a very small, very pointy breast. They don't know why the nurse is squeezing their little thigh and coming even closer, but they don't mind.

They've finally gotten comfortable, they've overcome the initial misgivings about the smell and general vibe of the joint, and figure if *you* trust these people, if you're comfortable enough to hand over your own flesh and blood to them, they must be A-OK.

Then the nurse stabs this spear into your infant's little virgin, heretofore undamaged skin. But the cries don't come right away. There's a small interval between Injection and Pain. Maybe it's that their little nerve endings take that much longer to transmit the news, but there's a good few, solid seconds where the baby doesn't register that they've just been savaged.

But *you* do. You know that with a jolt like that, a response will be forthcoming. I was painfully aware that there was a very short clock ticking, and only precious seconds of innocence remaining in my child's heart. Those beautiful, trusting, innocent eyes are about to transform horribly, and I have but a fleeting, minuscule window of opportunity to either distance myself from the event or soothe him; say something that will ready him, because any second now . . . and—*BAMMO!*—it hits. Wherever that shot was supposed to go, it just got there. And he is instantly, irrevocably *pissed*. Not regular pissed— rageful. There are no gradations. No transitional drama-award face. It doesn't hurt a Little, then a Little More, and then kind of Really, Really Hurt. It goes from Noth-ing Whatsoever to "OW OW OW OW OW OW OW OW OW OW OW OW OW OW OW OW" in a flash.

And then he whips his head in my direction.

"Did you SEE that?!"

You have nothing to offer except a colorful plastic key you pathetically shake around a little. This does nothing.

"Did you see what that lady did?! She just stabbed me!"

The betrayal is unspeakable.

"How could you let that happen? You were standing right there, you must have seen that, for crying out loud. You two are the worst parents I ever heard of. You're both cruel, untrustworthy, and no damn good . . . Now could somebody get me a Band-Aid? Do you think you could manage that?"

It killed me to know that I couldn't make his pain go away. I looked at him tenderly, thinking, "Son—"

"And don't think this hurts you more than it hurts me."

I thought, "Okay."

Look, a Fuzzy Tiger

To fully appreciate what having a baby does to your life, you need to really grasp the concept of Baby Time. Babies slow down time in *two* particularly exasperating ways.

First of all, things that used to take five minutes now take an hour. When you add a baby to any activity, even something as simple as Walking Out the Door, you must allow yourself one solid hour more than you used to. There's the packing, the changing, the planning for any one of seven hundred scenarios that could develop, and the going back for things you'd need for any of the two dozen *other* scenarios your spouse decided could happen because she heard of them happening to someone her friend knows.

This is why the moment your child is born, feel free to lose entirely from your vocabulary the phrase, "We'll be there in twenty minutes." It has no value, it has no more application. You will never again be anywhere in twenty minutes. Ever.

Furthermore, and this is the nasty *second* reality of Baby Time: Things that feel like they're taking an hour actually are *not*. I was once so proud of having successfully entertained my son for an entire afternoon. I designed and constructed an immense building-block fortress, played a vigorous round of "Where's-Daddy's-Nose?/Where-Are-Daddy's-Ears?" and rendered a poignant reading of *Harry the Hippo*, only to glance at my watch and discover that in fact *seven minutes* had elapsed.

BABIES SLOW DOWN TIME. Understand this. Accept it. Make friends with it. They tamper with the actual physics and mechanics of the Space/Time Continuum. In fact, if you play with a baby long enough, time will literally stop, and then go backward. These tiny people can actually *reverse* time. A friend of mine once played with his ten-month-old daughter for an entire afternoon, and by the time his wife came home, the man was seven years old. No kidding around, he was, astonishingly enough, a scant six or seven years older than his own child.

This is why parents love videos. Even the ones like me who swore, "I'm not going to be like all those parents who just drop their kid in front of the TV." Because you discover that videos have the power to *overcome* Baby Time. They are immune to the baby's unearthly powers. If the tape says "fifty-three minutes," you're going to get fifty-three minutes. Put the kid in front of that video, you are free to do fifty-three minutes' worth of stuff.

One time, the only tape I could find was the instructional video that came with our car. It was about thirty-five minutes long—which is exactly what I needed. As it turns out, my kid loved it. You know why? He'd never seen it. He's never seen *anything*.

And this is where the Powers That Be compensate nicely for the inconvenience of Baby Time. They throw in the wonderful Counter Force—Baby Point of View. One works against you, one helps you out.

Baby Point of View hinges on the simple premise that almost anything you show them, they've never seen before. And if they have, there's a very good chance they don't remember. So it is through this miracle that a piece of Scotch tape becomes the best toy ever made. A restaurant's fish tank becomes the San Diego Zoo. The produce department at the supermarket is suddenly the Wonderful Interactive Museum of Food—because it's all new.

It seems that the key parenting skill you need to develop when entertaining your new child is the ability to Distract. If they get bored, or scared, or cry for any reason, you just pull a sleight-of-hand and misdirect their simple little minds elsewhere. For starters, show them something. Anything.

"Look, a fuzzy tiger."

They will most likely stop crying and evaluate this new information.

"Hmm, a tiger . . . I hadn't realized that . . ."

"Yes, a tiger . . . look . . . see the tiger? . . ."

"Well, (*sniffle*) my stomach was hurting . . ."

"I know, I know . . ."

"But . . . a *tiger,* you say . . ."

"Yes, a tiger. Right here. Here is a tiger . . ."

It doesn't even have to be as interesting as a tiger. Any physical item that is currently on the planet and within reach will do.

"Look, the cap to Daddy's water bottle . . . see . . . plastic . . . and white . . . isn't that something? And here are some *keys.*"

It's truly a miracle that this works. I always expect them to demand more. At least an elaboration.

"Okay, I see . . . you're showing me keys . . . but what about them? Are they important? Do they open anything I should know about?"

"No . . ."

"So what are you telling me?"

"Um, nothing . . . just that they jingle . . . and they exist . . . and I have them right here."

"What do they have to do with my stomach ache?"

"Nothing, really."

"Then get out of here with that. Bring me a malted."

But they don't say that. They're willing to seriously consider whatever you have to offer.

Singing is also popular. Since the arrival of our child, I've been singing everything. Simple sentences like "I'm going to make your bottle now" become operatic arias, half spoken, half sung, and usually nasal, with randomly elongated vowels. Basically, everything sounds like Jerry

Lewis. So, "Who's crying?" becomes "Whoooooo's cryyyyyy—iiiinngggga fuuyymn?"

If a baby is on the verge of tears, sudden and emphatic singing directed right in their face will, nine out of ten times, do the trick.

"Twinkle, twinkle, liiit-tle star . . . how I wonder what you are . . ."

If they don't actually stop crying, they'll at least simmer down enough to see if you're any good. They'll listen to a few bars, and if you're *not* good, they'll resume crying. I mean, they may be easy, but they're not *that* easy.

Still, the fact that they even give you a *chance* is remarkable. That they have a legitimate grievance, and are willing to forgo complaining about it in exchange for a song, is, to me, darn decent of them.

This is something, again, that would not work at all with taller people. Try it. Next time your wife is upset about something, see what happens if you break into song.

"I can't believe you invited people over now. There is nothing in the house to eat . . ."

"Yes, but, honey, shh shhh, shhh, honey—look: *Seventy-six trom-bones led the big pa-rade . . .*"

"The place is a mess . . ."

". . . with a hun-dred-and-ten cornets right behind . . ."

Beat.

"Oh, I guess it's okay . . ."

It'd never work. But babies, fortunately, are more easily sidetracked.

.   .   .

Infants are also, I've discovered, quite fond of the "peekaboo" game. The game is simply: Show them your face, then take it away. It's essentially two components: "I'm here," and "then I'm not." "I'm suddenly right in front of you, then mysteriously, not-so-much." It's the *change* they like. The alternation of being there and then not being there. And while you're *not* there, they enjoy the anticipation of you coming right back in two seconds. (The first four hundred times you do it gives them a sense of the pattern.)

Ironically, while my son seems to love the "faces coming at him" more than the "faces going away," I seem to recall that *I* was just the opposite. When I was a baby, I preferred the part of "peekaboo" where they went *away*. I didn't like the "peek" as much as the "aboo." I was a big fan of the "aboo," the "stop sneaking up on me and just sit over there" aspect of the game. But that may very well be just me.

There are times, however, that as easily as kids can be amused, the sheer burden of being the one doing the amusing can be overwhelming. Especially if you're doing the amusing all by yourself.

One time, my precious little tax deduction and I were having great fun playing. But after an hour or so, I realized there's only so much playing I'm capable of doing. I'm not *that* inventive, *that* enthusiastic, *that* naturally playful. I mean, I can indicate the inventory of toys available, demonstrate how the sliding things slide and the bouncy things bounce, all of which he will either try himself or put in his mouth until the toy is so dense with saliva absorption that it falls to the floor and the game is over. But then what? No matter how much you worship and adore your child, there are times that you hit your limit. You look at your watch, calculate the astonishingly large block of time left to fill, and realize, "I'm not going to make it."

This, I discovered, is what they mean when they say you *have a child*. You literally *have* him. There is no other verb operating. You're not "doing," you're not "being," you're not "interacting," you're not in any way benefiting from each other—you simply "have" the child. Much in the same way that you *have* a blue blazer.

"You have kids?"

"Yup, we have two kids. One in high school, one a freshman in college."

"Do you have a blue blazer?"

"Yes, upstairs, in the closet, on the right."

You may not be wearing the blazer, or in any way entertaining the blazer, but that blue blazer is nonetheless yours. The main difference, of course, is that not every baby goes with gray slacks.

Hey, There's Milk
in There

"You're scared of my breasts, aren't you?"

"I'm not scared . . ."

"Then why are you skittish around them?"

"Who's *skittish*? No one's being *skittish* . . ."

Here's the truth: That milk can flow from a breast is, no question about it, a miraculous miracle. Breasts that heretofore had no experience in this area suddenly, upon the birth of a child, start serving up the one item this particular child likes to eat. Talk about packing your own lunch—this guy not only sees to it that he'll have what he needs when he lands, he's arranged for someone else's body to dispense it upon request.

But as miraculous and moving as this is, I can't get past the fact that *food* is coming out of my wife's breasts. What was once essentially an entertainment center has now become a juice bar. This takes some getting used to. It's like if *bread* were suddenly coming out of a person's neck. Wouldn't that be unsettling? Let's say you're a woman. If you were nibbling your husband's ear and came away with a piece of toast, wouldn't you be a tad skittish? That's all I'm saying.

My son never had this concern. He and my wife developed a terrifically fine-tuned routine. Whenever he felt like nursing, he would look up at her and shoot her a very seductive little Marcello Mastroianni glance, and in response, she would put a breast in his mouth.

It was that simple. He knew what he wanted, *she* knew what he wanted, no words need be exchanged. And it's amazing to witness how swiftly and inconspicuously nursing mamas can lift their shirts, slide open their bras, and maneuver both baby and breast into full operating mode in a matter of seconds.

My wife and child got so good at it, there were times we were in mid-conversation, and I didn't even know it was going on. I'd be talking to my wife, looking at her, she's looking at me, absolutely involved in the discussion, when I'd suddenly hear a slurping noise from inside her shirt.

"Man, you guys are good. I didn't even know the baby was in the room."

And it's not the easiest thing in the world to conceal. I know if it were me and I had, for example, a raccoon licking molasses off my stomach, I don't know that I could sit on a couch and look you in the eyes like nothing was going on.

When your wife nurses your child several times a day, it's perfectly understandable to overlook the intimacy of the act and behave as if indeed nothing was going on. However, when you're in the presence of a woman *not* your wife nursing a child *not* your own, the protocol can get murky. Plenty of times we'll have friends over who have a new baby, and the mom will slap that baby onto her breast, and to be quite honest with you, I'm never sure exactly where to look. You don't want to make her self-conscious and run out of the room in the name of discretion, but you also don't want to be so blasé that you stand there chatting about how many channels you think you get with a satellite dish, while someone you frequently have dinner with has her breast out and about in your living room.

Here's what I've decided: You can stay in the room as long as you keep yourself busy and moving around, so your eyes never fall directly onto the nursing mom and child. If they *do* land there, you may look only at her *neck*, or any point north. You start looking below her neck, you're looking for trouble.

Furthermore (and this may be way more information than you need), even if you catch a glimpse of the woman's breast, you're still potentially okay as long as it's the *fleshy* part of the breast. The Bosom at Large, as it were. If the baby jerks away suddenly to reveal the actual working mechanics of the nursing distribution setup, you

must, out of sheer decency, get out of there. Start scratch-
ing your eyes like you're having a violent hay-fever attack
or something. Turn around and pretend the back of your
pants are itching, and tug at your belt for a while until
she has time to gather herself properly. And then pretend
like nothing happened.

Now *That's* Funny

I'll never forget the day I got the first real, genuine laugh out of my son. I don't remember anything in my life feeling that good. It was just so intoxicating and heart-warming that I'd like to have that laugh bottled and put into an I.V. that drips into me endlessly.

When he hadn't laughed for the first few months, I just decided I wasn't funny. It must be my fault; I'm trying to make him laugh, he's not laughing, it's me. It never dawned on me that he just wasn't ready.

For the first few months, you get nothing. Then you get smiles. Actually, not "smiles" per se, but little cheek spasms that *look* like smiles and in fact are him wincing as a pocket of gas rockets through his torso. Sometimes it's not even that; they're just arbitrary, uncontrolled twitches that, when you're hoping for a smile, you decide are "close enough."

Then, after a while, you start to get actual smiles, and you learn the difference. You get a real smile and you can't believe your good fortune. I'm not sure why it's such a big deal. I'd hate to think I'm really that desperate for approval. What it is, I've decided, is the first sign that you're actually getting through; that this is not just two interplanetary beings staring at each other. With that smile, you know that *they* know you're out there.

But it becomes addictive. In no time, that smile is no longer enough. You need more. You need—the Laugh. And you'll do anything to get it. You make faces, funny noises. You animate dolls and produce entire one-act plays around them. You talk high, you talk low. You mock the child's mother in her presence, hoping to parlay one laugh into two. There is nothing you won't try.

Ironically, the first laugh I got came from doing something that I had been doing for months: a simple raspberry on the belly. This has different names in different families: Slurpies, Bloweys, Churtles, Normans—all basically an intense compression of air from the lips-of-an-adult against the stomach-of-a-child, resulting in the amusingly loud, disruptive, faux-fart effect.

At first, I didn't know for sure I was getting the laugh. I was holding the kid up in the air, showing off for company, my face implanted deep into his rib cage to make sure the raspberry was registering. The noise was so loud and forceful that to my ears, it was drowning out the laugh. Everyone else in the room had a clear view and was having a ball. I would hear them laugh in response to his laugh, pull my head up to see, but by the time I got there, the laugh was over. It was a little unfair, actually, seeing as how I was the one doing all the work. I would "raspberry" faster and shorter, trying to get back up in time to catch the laugh. But I kept missing it. Sort of like standing up to get a good look at your lap: It's gone before you get there.

But then, it happened—the monumental and glorious breakthrough. I coaxed from my son a sustained laugh, saw it and heard it with my own eyes and ears, and—I just wanted to dive in and spend my entire lifetime in the fluffy cloud of that moment.

And I couldn't help wondering why this wasn't funny to him the first few thousand times I did it. Why now? Why wasn't it amusing January through May? I decided that in the beginning, it doesn't matter how amusing anything is; if you're three days old, you're just not in the mood to laugh. The machinery is there. The wiring that will let you laugh is installed at birth, but it's sort of like cable; someone has to turn it on. It needs to be initialized and activated and then, hopefully, it should keep working forever.

Of course some people grow up and *stop* laughing, and it's entirely possible that if you lift up their shirts and give them a raspberry, they'll start laughing, too. However, I don't know these people, and I don't really feel it's my place to blow on their bellies.

Make Room
for Daddy

If I'm not mistaken, there was a time, not long ago, when I actually had a *name*. When you become a daddy, "Daddy" becomes your name.

"Daddy's going to make you breakfast."

"Daddy wants to give you a kiss."

"No, don't put that in your mouth—give the dead bird to Daddy."

I was never crazy about people who talk about themselves in the third person. To me, it's an affectation reserved for superstar athletes ("Dennis Rodman's not happy with how Dennis Rodman played tonight") or dim-witted nutcases in bad movies ("Johnny no like to strangle puppies, but Johnny *confused*").

With babies, however, I can understand that their brains may not be ready to distinguish among so many pronouns, names, and nicknames, so it's best to just give everyone *one* name and then stick with that.

"Mommy loves you."

"Mommy has to go now."

"Mommy is so tired, Mommy could literally cry at any given second."

Where it starts to sour is when Mommy and Daddy use these names to refer to each other and start talking *through* the child.

"Tell Mommy that Daddy's going to go out and be back in half an hour."

"Could you ask Daddy where he's going?"

"Tell Mommy Daddy's going to pick up a paper and a Snickers bar."

"Ask Daddy why he doesn't take you with him so Mommy can take a shower."

"Tell Mommy that maybe Daddy was *going* to say that, but Mommy just didn't give Daddy a chance."

After several months of being "Daddy" and "Mommy," we found that we couldn't shake the habit. We referred to ourselves in the third person even when the baby wasn't around.

"What was the name of that Chinese restaurant Daddy and Mommy loved downtown?"

"Szechuan Garden?"

"Yeah. Mommy wants to get some fried rice from Szechuan Garden."

Creepier still is when you start talking to yourself *about*

yourself in the third person. I was home alone one morning, walked into the bathroom, and announced to no one,
"Daddy's going to brush his teeth."

It's impossible to stop. I walked into my office and
actually said, "Hold all Daddy's calls, please."

People look at you like you're nuts.

There was a point, though, where I started to enjoy it.
It did have a bit of a sense of *grandeur*. I walked around
like Burl Ives in *Cat on a Hot Tin Roof*.

"Big Daddy's gone down in the basement . . . Nobody
bother Big Daddy."

Because, when you think about it, being a "Daddy" is
not just a name; it's a *title*. Like "Duke" or "Baron." And
like any self-respecting title, it comes with certain privi-
leges.

"Daddy knows best."

"Why? Because Daddy said so."

"Daddy has had a really rough day, so all in the Kingdom shall be still, as Daddy has to lie down for a little
nap."

Stepping Out with My Baby

When you have a brand-new child, your world shrinks. With the exception of going to get food and more diapers, you don't step out of the house. In time, of course, the three of you do venture out. Or Mommy and baby venture out. And finally, Daddy has to go out with baby—alone.

In terms of responsibility and potential for error, this is light-years beyond taking care of the very same kid at home, comfortably ensconced within the confines of your familiar, relatively safe walls. It's yet another *next step*.

I didn't even realize I hadn't gone out until a new-dad friend of mine and I started comparing notes.

"You been alone with the kid yet?"

"Of course. Lots of times."

"You gone outside?"

I said, "Sure."

"With the kid?"

"Yeah, with the kid. What's the big deal?"

"You're telling me you've been outside with the kid, on the street, around strangers, in the world?"

And it hit me.

"Oh, *outside* outside. I thought you meant like in the backyard . . . Out in the world? Oh, no. I'm not ready for anything like *that*."

I did know the day was coming; you can't put off something like that forever. Not surprisingly, the push came from my wife.

"I'd really love to take a nap."

"By all means," I said. "Go ahead. I got the baby. We'll watch a video or something."

"It's a beautiful day out . . ."

"Oh, it sure is," I countered, grabbing the nearest video, fearing where this was headed.

"Why don't you take him out for a stroll?"

I got a little sweaty.

"In the stroller?"

"Yes, in the stroller. Take him for a stroll, in the stroller."

"Where would we go?"

"Why don't you take him down to the mailbox?" my wife suggested perkily.

"The *mailbox*?"

"Yeah, there's three envelopes by the door that have to go out today. You guys could mail them together. It'll be like an adventure."

Okay, here's another way to know you have a baby: Going to the mailbox is now an "adventure." With no baby, "the mailbox" is not a *destination*. It's not even a *somewhere*. It's a twenty-second pause on the *way* to somewhere. But with a child, you need to always be going somewhere, doing something. Every mundane chore gets elevated to adventure status. And not just because of the sheer amount of preparation—the aforementioned Baby Time. It's because you need to *believe* you're on an adventure. You need that veneer of excitement. The illusion of purpose. The grand sense of accomplishment. After all, if you thought all you were doing was "watching the baby," you might feel a bit unchallenged. Or—and you never heard it from me—bored. If, however, you take this responsibility and dress it up with a little goal, a tiny task, a splash of destination, why—now you've got something. Now you've got yourself an Adventure.

So, off to the mailbox we go. But first, a quick inventory of provisions: Diaper bag? Check. Blanket? Check. Sun hat? Sunblock? Little red corduroy clown with the terry-cloth head he enjoys biting? Check, check, and check. Load up, roll out, company ho!

Once you push that stroller outside, it's a whole new world.

"Hey, there's cars here . . . Who are all these people

driving around? And look, there's other people walking around, too. Right by me and the stroller, for crying out loud! Running and hurrying and coughing and bumping—I don't like this one bit."

Halfway down the block, a woman walked by and stopped to admire my child. Now, I must admit, I have mixed feelings about strangers ogling my baby. Obviously, I love hearing how beautiful he is. I'm even gullible enough to believe that when they say he's the cutest baby they've ever seen, they really mean it. I maintain they have an up-to-date record of other children they've seen over the years, and running a quick tally, they can calculate that he is indeed tangibly cuter than all the others.

In fact, if someone walks by and *doesn't* notice how remarkably attractive my child is, I feel hurt and insulted. I have to restrain myself from catching up to them and asking them if they're sure they don't want to look again. But usually I decide that there must be a good reason. Maybe they're in a very bad mood. Or, more likely, their children had been stolen by dingoes like in that Meryl Streep movie, so to stop and admire my child, though certainly their inclination, would be, ultimately, too painful for them. So, that's probably why they didn't say anything.

But my addiction to admiration aside, I don't really know who these people are. They could be nuts. Or carrying germs incurable since the fourteen hundreds—I have no way of knowing.

Fortunately, this lady seemed to pose no threat. She

smiled from a safe distance, made a few friendly baby sounds to engage my son, and then mentioned to me that though she had traveled the world extensively for many years, she had never seen or heard mention of a child being quite this splendid looking, and then went on her way. I was very proud. And felt my confidence increase. I thought for sure this lady was stopping us to point out that I was doing something wrong: The kid's leg was hanging out of the stroller, his little seat belt was undone, or he was buckled in upside down—*something* wrong.

But to my surprise, she said nothing of the sort. And as I walked along, past other people, nobody said anything like that. Nobody criticized me, nobody made suggestions. There were no critical stares, no looks that said, "Hey, look at that guy over there, with the stroller . . . Something's not right . . . He doesn't know how to work the stroller . . . Why, he's not a father at all . . . That man is an impostor . . . Police! Somebody! Stop that man!"

But nothing. As far as they knew, I was just "some guy out with his kid." A certified Dad. They're oblivious to the cold sweat, the white-knuckle grip I have on the stroller handle. No one notices that each time I get to a new sidewalk, I actually bend and lift the entire carriage up and over the curb, because secretly I'm afraid I might tilt it too far and slide my offspring into the gutter. God bless them, they notice none of this. Even my baby doesn't notice. (Although at one intersection, after I carried the stroller—*with the kid in it*—in my arms for a block and a half because it looked to me like some guy was possibly going to spit, I did notice my son look up at me from his forty-five-degree perch as if to say, "Are you sure we don't want to get Mom in on this? She's very good at just this type of thing.")

I was thrilled to know that all this was merely my own private nightmare, and whatever shortcomings I may or may not have are nobody's business.

But as I thought about it, a new concern came to mind.

"If they can't tell I don't know what I'm doing, how do I know *they* know what *they're* doing? Maybe we're all impostors." Suddenly I was looking at the world with new eyes. Very frightened eyes.

"What if *nobody* knows what they're doing? When I sit down in a restaurant and a waitress asks me what I want, how do I know she actually works there? Maybe she's just a lunatic who showed up with an apron and a pad of paper, and no one has the guts to ask her to leave. When you get on a plane, how do you know the pilot has ever actually flown before? Who's to say he's not a luggage handler who swiped a better uniform? Is it not entirely possible that when our obstetrician was in medical school, his nickname was "Goofball"?

I soon realized this was a very unhealthy train of thought to be on, and I jumped right off the train. I focused my concentration instead on the job at hand—taking my son to the mailbox. But it did change the way I look at people. And it certainly made me marvel at my wife, who, apparently, goes out with the kid every day as if it were nothing.

.   .   .

Finally we arrive at the mailbox—an exhausting block and a half from home. Dizzy with the victory of arriving at our destination in more or less one piece, I reach into my pocket, retrieve the now sweaty envelopes, and am about to toss them into the mailbox when I hear a voice. It's my wife's voice, echoing God-like in my head.

"Talk to him."

"Hmm?" I say automatically, totally accepting that my wife might in fact be physically standing next to me, just for a follow-up evaluation on my performance.

"Talk to him. Explain to him what you're doing," the voice in my head suggests.

Sometimes I forget that part—talking to my child. Actually *being* with him. When I'm in charge of the kid, I tend to either stare at him like he's television or drift totally into a world of my own, running through my list of things-I-have-to-do-later-when-I'm-not-taking-care-of-the-kid. Or I take the job *so* seriously I become blinded by the severity of the responsibility, and panic. What I seem to miss is the middle ground—the part where you share, teach, learn, play—the part you can actually enjoy.

"Right. Talk to him. I'll do that. Thanks," I say to myself, and the voice of the Nice Lady in My Head leaves me alone again.

"So," I say to my buckled-up Beautiful Boy. "This is a mailbox."

And in response, he takes a hearty bite out of his little red corduroy clown's terry-cloth head.

"See? Daddy's going to put these letters into the mail-box. See? . . . What else can I tell you . . . The mailbox is blue."

When in doubt, mention the color. They can't get enough of colors, these kids.

"It's a blue mailbox."

Another ferocious bite-and-tug almost removes the corduroy clown's left ear. Clearly the boy is not that in-terested—I'll just mail the damn letters.

"Explain to him how it works."

"I tried."

"Try again."

"All right, all right. Quit yelling."

Fortunately, no one sees or hears this violent exchange in my head. (See what I mean? They think I'm a guy-with-his-kid, and in fact I'm not only hearing voices but barking back at them.)

"We put the letters in the mailbox, and then the mail-man comes and gets them."

Talking to your baby is a lot like being on a first date; you feel like you're either saying too little or too much.

"The postal system was invented by Benjamin Frank-lin. In Philadelphia. He also invented bifocals. And I hear he had over one hundred illegitimate children."

Probably too much.

"The mailman takes the letters and puts them in a big bag and then he takes them to where they're going. See, this one goes to Aunt Ellen, who sent you that itchy sweater you hate, and this one goes to the Electricity

Company so they don't shut off our electricity and force us out of our home."

A little too heavy.

"Forget that. That will never happen."

Then, remembering that Demonstrating is always better than Explaining, I unbuckle him, scoop him up, and illustrate my letter-mailing technique.

"What you want to do is: Pull down the handle, open the mailbox's mouth, and then you *flick* the letters in. You want to get that nice flicking motion in your wrist . . . And then you pull the mouth open-and-closed a few times, to make sure the letters went down. A lot of people will tell you that doesn't do anything. They're wrong. You *must* check. Otherwise the mailbox will chew up your letter and stick it in a corner where no one can find it for years and years and years."

My son smiles. I pull the handle up and down again. He seems to enjoy the squeaky noise. Who said mailboxes aren't a dynamite activity for youngsters?

As we prepare for our return voyage, I wonder if I've left anything out.

"Now, you may notice, it says here they pick up at eleven A.M., but between you and me it says the same thing on every mailbox, and there's no way that the guy can be at every mailbox in town at the same time, so I say just throw it in whenever you feel like it—it makes no difference. But you know what? You probably won't be mailing things by yourself for a while, so forget that. The main thing for you to remember, I would say, is: The box is blue. It's a big shiny blue box with a squeaky blue mouth."

As I buckle him back in, my son gives me one of those magnificent, otherworldly smiles, and looks at me as if to say, "Dad, I don't know what you're talking about, but you seem like a very nice man."

Meanwhile, Back at the Office

The moment you have a baby, every available wall space and square inch of surface area is covered with baby pictures. Big pictures, little pictures, pictures in frames, pictures thumbtacked to the wall . . . you name it. For a while, we were actually buying new furniture just so we had more surfaces on which to put more pictures.

Even though I used to make fun of people who thrust their children's photos in your face against your will, and swore up and down that I would never become one of those people, I have in fact become not just "one" of those people—I became the *president* of all those people.

When I returned to the office as a dad, no one was safe. Anyone who wasn't smart enough or quick enough to get out of the way was cornered and detained for as long as it took to study my baby's picture and reiterate

what I already knew to be the case: This child is prepos-
terously cute.

Being out of the house and back in the office made me
feel even better about being a dad. Because at the office
you get all the accolades for being a dad without any of
the actual responsibility. At home, everyone is so busy in
the nitty-gritty business of *being* a parent, there's no time
for back-slapping adulation.

But if you walk around the office showing pictures of
your baby and talking about how fun/exciting/hard/
challenging/different it all is, what can anyone say but
"Boy, it sounds like you're a great dad."

And you get to gush in modesty.

"Well, I just do the best I can."

Unlike your home life, which has, upon the arrival of
your child, changed forever in every way conceivable,
your office has remained the same. There's no new, red-
and-yellow plastic furniture for you to trip over; people
aren't walking around like sleep-deprived zombies;
they're not speaking in strained, hushed tones. Your office—a place which ordinarily you're dying to flee the
first moment you can—is suddenly all the more appeal-
ing, specifically *because* it has simply remained unchanged.
The familiarity is soothing.

One day shortly after my son's birth, I found myself
remaining in my office after hours, sitting in my familiar
desk chair, gazing at one of the eleven hundred pictures

of my boy I had surrounded myself with, and just mar-
veling. I marveled at how soft and round his face is, how
wet and little his little wet lips are. I was almost to the
point of taking out a pencil and physically counting all
my blessings when a friend came in.

"What are you still doing here?"

"Huh? Oh, nothing. C'mere . . . Look at this picture . . . have you ever seen anything sweeter?"

"No, I haven't."

"You're darn right you haven't . . . Boy, I'll tell you,
there's nothing like a kid to remind you what's important
in this world, huh?"

"So true."

"Seriously . . . *work* is not important, *money's* not important—just family, and children, and . . ."

"So why don't you go home?"

"How's that?"

"I say, why don't you get out of here and go home
and *be* with that family of yours?"

"Oh . . ."

Good question.

What I *didn't* say was, "Because this is actually easier.
It's much easier to be a perfect dad from a distance . . ."

If you asked them, almost everyone would say that, indeed, Family is more important than Work. They may
not *act* accordingly, but they at least claim to embrace the
thought as a guiding principle of their lives.

And while I believe it to be true myself, I'm not sure

it needs to be the truth for *everybody*. I think it kind of depends on what you do.

What if you're a genius? Or a world leader? Isn't it more important that you lead the world than get home on time? If you're Albert Einstein, couldn't you effectively argue that discovering the theory of relativity and unraveling the mysteries of the universe may have more value than promptly sitting down to supper at six?

I don't know if, for example, Mozart actually had kids, but certainly there is no record of him ever leaving the office early to coach Peewee Soccer League.

And even if he *was* a terrible father—do we really care? Let's say, worst-case scenario, Mozart *ignored* his kids. Just totally ignored them. Never went home, worked feverishly into the night, slept at his desk, woke up, picked up that big feather pen, and started working again. In retrospect, wouldn't you rather have the extra string quartet? Wouldn't you say that the emotional well-being of one twelve-year-old Austrian kid is a small price to pay for *The Marriage of Figaro*? Now, certainly I feel bad for the kid, and if I was his friend I'm sure I'd have said, "You're right, man . . . your dad stinks." But as a society, isn't Mozart staying late at the office, checking for mistakes in a bassoon concerto, more of a contribution than reading *Runaway Bunny* to a European toddler?

I would argue maybe it is, but unlike Mozart, I have to go home and give my baby a bath.

The Baby
and the Bathwater

One of my favorite baby activities, which can also virtually qualify as a *sport,* is Bathing. Giving a baby a bath combines some of the most challenging elements of swimming, gymnastics, sculling, and fishing, as well as being a thorough cardiovascular workout for the sweating parent.

You wouldn't think that a person weighing roughly the same as a moderate-sized sea bass could be this difficult to control in water, but water has a phenomenal effect on babies. Their muscles expand to fifty times their normal strength and can exhaust even the most well-conditioned athlete, let alone wiped-out parents who are too depleted even to look for their gym shorts.

Baby Baths are very different from Grown-up Baths. When a baby sits in a bath, there's nothing either medi-

tative or hygienic about it. Little attention is paid to scrubbing or relaxing. The key agendas are as follows: For the
baby, floating, moving, and tossing as many rubber and
foam toys as you can within the time allowed, while getting as much water as possible *outside* the designated tub
area. And for you, to avoid all of the several hundred ways
in which your child can make you race them to an emergency room.

In addition to the countless hard surfaces that shout of
potential danger, there is also the *water* factor. Water is a
funny element. In a glass, water is your friend. It cools
you down, wets your whistle—that kind of water isn't
going to hurt anybody. But pile it up in a tub, it gets
crazy. It gangs up with the other water, surrounds your
baby, and just *dares you* to screw up. When bathing a
young person, you can't turn your back on that water for
an instant.

The compensation for this high-intensity nerve-fest,
however, is that when it's all over, you get to look at a
spanking-clean American.

And there's not much that can compare to a just-out-
of-the-bath baby. Once you get past the last hurdle—
getting them in a towel while they slither and squirm out
of your arms like a robust salmon, you get to look at that
face peeking through their terry cloth shrink-wrap and
inhale this giggly, squeaky, rosy, shampoo-smelling baby.

I particularly enjoy a baby with perfectly combed wet
hair. It gives him a look of confidence and savoir faire,

as if he passed a mirror and said, "Hang on there, hand-some." And then whipped out a little pocket comb and styled his hair to look like a parakeet's head.

This is one of those times when you want to literally *eat the baby up* in several ravenous gulps. I was once hold-ing my shiny-perfect, postbath son in my arms and started gumming his neck, trying hard to not ingest him entirely, and I noticed *he* was busy holding his favorite yellow ducky in his fist and gumming *that* for all he was worth. And suddenly I understood why babies put everything in their mouths: When you love something *so* much, there is no way you can properly convey the power of your affection short of devouring and consuming it wholly. It's an animal instinct that is triggered not by rage or hunger but only by a love that is limitless and beyond reason. (To buy into this theory, of course, you must ignore the fact that there is virtually nothing a baby *wouldn't* put in its mouth. But still, I think you know what I'm saying.)

Babies. You just gotta kiss them. The funny thing is, for all the time I spend kissing my baby, I'm not even sure he particularly likes it. Or knows what it is. To an infant, a kiss is probably a vague sense of "This person likes me, certainly wishes me no harm," combined with "Boy, he sure likes to stand close."

Or maybe even, "I don't know why he's wasting his time with me when there is a perfectly good yellow ducky right here."

Boy Meets Dog

For many years, our dog had a very cushy job. He lived in a nice house, had his own designated chair to sleep in, had not one but *two* doting, loving, grown-up humans who without fail (okay—*almost* without fail) made it their business to feed him, walk him, scratch him, buy chewy toys, and generally take care of his every need. In exchange, he had merely to look cute, be furry, periodically retrieve a tennis ball, and—and this is the important one—try really hard to not take a dump on the carpets. And even if he *did* besmirch an irreplaceable rug that used to belong to my grandmother's mother, he knew that after a few minutes of yelling on our part and some long-eyed, sorrowful looks on his part, everything would be forgiven and life would return to its rosy self. His position was secure; he was the Child of the House.

Boom! Enter an actual child, and see how quickly that changes. Instantly, the hierarchy and social order of a dog's universe are irreparably and permanently thrown askew.

The moment we returned home carrying our newborn child, our dog became—for the first time in his life—a dog. He took a huge tumble down the evolutionary ladder. The days of trying to pass himself off as just-another-member-of-the-family-who-happens-to-be-able-to-lick-himself-into-a-pretzel were now over.

The poor thing should have seen it coming. The writing was on the walls. Month after month of deteriorating Quality Time. Walks overlooked. Treats distributed with less frequency and far less enthusiasm . . . Something was clearly amiss.

Some people I know actually tried to prepare their dog for the Big Day by bringing home baby clothes and baby toys for the dog to smell. The theory was that by breeding a sense of familiarity, the dog wouldn't be shocked by the infant's arrival and, more importantly, wouldn't attack it in the driveway. Now, while you certainly have to admire this kind of forethought, who's going to do that? You don't do it for any other guests that come by. You never say, "Brandy, next week the Gendlemans are coming for dinner, so just so you won't be thrown, here's a pair of their pants. These are actual slacks worn only yesterday by Mr. Gendleman. And for dessert, here's a pair of socks from the Mrs."

Chances are, the dog will adjust. But keep in mind, though they can *sense* change, they can't always determine exactly what the change *is*. For example, when our son came home, the dog definitely knew something was up. All the attention that used to be his was now spent on the newcomer, which, as far as the dog could make out, was a nicely wrapped blanket. That's all he could see. A faint blue blur that was whisked past his head, handed from person to person with the utmost care, and never once placed below dog's-eye level. The only conclusion he could come to was, "Boy, they sure love that blanket . . . I've never seen anything like it . . . They're protecting that blanket with their lives . . . Hey, maybe there's something valuable inside the blanket . . . I bet it's wrapped around roast beef."

When our child finally did emerge from the blanket, the dog used his standard approach to anything new: "Is it Foe, Friend, or Food?" The three F's into which everything in a dog's world can be categorized.

At first, the dog was cautious; perhaps this alien creature could harm him. He sniffed, prodded, and circled until information was gathered.

When he realized that Blanket Boy was no Foe, the clever pooch switched to his other primary instinct and stared at the baby with just one thought on his simple mind:

"Maybe I could eat him. He's soft and chubby and, if I'm not mistaken, currently sleeping."

One time, I was looking after my newborn child, who was sleeping blissfully in one of the seventy-three seating contraptions we now had, when from the corner of my eye I noticed the dog creeping slowly toward the baby, dragging himself by the elbows like an infantryman in a bad World War II movie. When he finally got there, his head hovering alarmingly close to my only child, I saw— or thought I saw—the dog's jaws open to reveal a flash of canine incisors, and I will tell you this: Though I'm not necessarily known for my speed and agility, if the Olympics had a "hurl-a-Labrador-across-a-living-room" event, I would've done very well. Even the dog was impressed. As he ricocheted off a cushy armchair, he looked at me as if to say, "I had no idea you could do that."

I immediately took him aside, apologized, and tried to explain the regulations inherent in our new Dog/Human Being contract. He seemed to understand. He at least knew enough to pretend to understand so as to win a free piece of cheese.

Shortly thereafter, he did indeed adjust. He finally made Friends with the baby. When he approached, he did so with respect and caution. He lapped at the baby with big, loving doggie licks. And when informed he couldn't lick the face, he restricted himself to arms and legs. (Or, as they appeared in his mind, "the drumsticks.") He even took to sleeping under the crib, growling gentle warnings when anyone but us wandered too close to the boy. My wife and I beamed with pride as he began to tag along wherever we carried the baby, plopping himself down at every stop. We were thrilled to see the affection and concern he consistently displayed. However, when we noticed that at mealtimes he was not only predictably right alongside the high chair but actually brought his own knife and fork, we understood the truth: He was looking for food. After seeing the baby eat often enough, he knew that by simply being in the right place at the right time, he could score a nice array of fruits, vegetables, applesauce, and stray crackers. Between the stuff bouncing off the baby's face or dripping from his chin, and the fistfuls of goodies thrown down like sticky manna from heaven, our child had become essentially a Dog Buffet. An all-you-can-drop salad bar.

So even if the baby turned out not to be *actual* food, he at least was a generous dispenser of food. If not a food source, certainly a nice source of food.

And to a dog, that's really what friends are for.

Why Dads Aren't Moms

There was a period, when our son was still brand-new, when I walked around beaming with pride in my new role as father, but could also, on that very same day, totally forget that I had a kid at all.

I'd be in a casual conversation with someone and they'd say, "Do you have kids yourself?"

And I'd say, "Nope . . . No, *wait*—I do, I do . . . yes, we have a son. He's six weeks old, and I love him more than anything in the world. I forgot . . . Would you like to see a picture?"

My wife has no such memory lapses. There is never an instant when she is not thinking about, talking about, or in some way connected, on an organic, cellular level, to the child she so artfully bore. And it's beyond her comprehension that the child's *other* parent isn't the same way.

Time after time, I was confronted with evidence suggesting that, try though I might, I wasn't as naturally gifted a parent as my wife. We may both love our child with equal passion, but she was better at doing something about it. Still, I refused to accept defeat. I was determined to be the Best Parent Anyone Ever Heard Of. Or at least as good as her.

But it wasn't easy. This girl was good. For example, my son's mother can, at any point in the day, tell you precisely what he ate, how much, how recently, and how long it took him to eat it. I can't really do that.

Now, in partial defense of my gender, I think some of this innate talent is related to women's ability to breast-feed. It certainly helps to keep you connected to your child if your body parts swell up and ache whenever the kid is hungry. I suspect that if five minutes before my child was due for a sandwich, I got a persistent throbbing in my testicles, I'd be more on top of things, too.

To compensate for my lack of natural gift, I turned to Science. I bought an absurdly complicated watch for the express purpose of timing all child-related data. And for a few days, I was like NASA. I could give you readings accurate to several hundred decimal points as well as open up the trash compactor on *Apollo 12*. I started timing everything. I was hitting that start button so many times, I began to lose track of what it was I was timing. I'd hand the baby over to my wife and prepare for the briefing.

"Did he eat? How long has he been up? Does he need to be changed?"

I'd proudly check my watch.

"It just so happens that exactly three hours, thirty-eight minutes, and twelve-point-five seconds ago . . . um . . . *something* happened. I don't know exactly what. But it's been going on for quite some time, I'll tell you that."

As this was not the first time I was unable to provide the information requested, my wife—the no-nonsense Headmistress of the School of Our Recent Child—paused, shook her head, and remarked, "You just don't get it, do you?"

Okay, first of all, let me tell you how much that particular sentence bugs me. From anyone.

"You just don't get it."

They haven't yet invented a conversation stopper more offensive, more hostile, or more completely dismissive. And it's become quite popular. You hear it all over the place. At work, in social situations, in the midst of the most amiable discourse, a difference of opinion is discovered, and it all comes to a crashing halt with someone declaring that someone else "just doesn't get it."

The implication is "I don't care enough to explain this any other way. And furthermore, it's my contention that you are literally impaired intellectually to the point that you do not get things that, to almost everyone else, are quite evident."

It's all the more irritating coming from the one person you would think *likes* you; who would think that the two of you "get" the same things. Which is kind of why you're together in the first place.

And there's not even a decent comeback line for "You just don't get it." What can you say?

"Oh, I get it. I just . . . I just . . . I just don't get it *right now*."

Sensing that she had hit a frayed nerve, my wife softened.

"Maybe we're just different," she said.

"Who?"

"You . . . me . . . men . . . women . . . maybe   we're just different."

Suddenly, I felt so relieved.

"Okay," I thought. "Maybe that's it. Maybe she can do things that I can't, just like I can do some things maybe *she* can't . . . We may be different . . ."

I sure liked that better than "You just don't get it."

And while I certainly wasn't going to stop trying to get better at this Dad thing, I felt liberated from having to master it by lunch.

Tough Love

In the beginning, whatever creative sleeping schedule your baby makes up, you accept. If they like to sleep in the morning and be up all night, fine. After all, they just arrived on the planet, their clocks are bound to be screwed up for a while.

But after a few months, for the sake of the child's development—not to mention your own sanity—you have to take matters into your own hands.

"Look, you've been here long enough to know this is the way it works: We're up in the morning and we sleep at night—which you'll remember is the *dark* part of the day. If you want to take a nap or two in the afternoon, that's fine. But basically, them's the rules, and you better straighten up and fly right."

Traditionally, their response is: "Hey, I could give a

crap about your rules. These are *my* rules, so why don't *you* get with the program?"

And thus ensues a hideous tug-of-war in which everybody loses.

The first hurdle was the "Does the baby sleep in bed with us or in his own bed?" discussion.

There are strong arguments for both. Initially, we loved the idea of all sleeping in one big familial bed, but soon discovered that between the baby waking us up and then having to sleep on eggshells so as to not wake him or roll right over him, the net result was we weren't sleeping all that great.

On the other hand, when he's in the next room screaming at four in the morning and one of you has to stumble out of your warm bed to deal with it, it seems a lot more desirable to have him lying between you so all you have to do is simply flop a lazy arm across his pajamas and pat him back to sleep from deep within your *own* sleep. But we were determined to do things the "right way." We read the books, we asked around.

It turns out there's a popular school of thought that maintains the best thing you can do for your child is to teach them to soothe *themselves* to sleep. In short—let 'em cry. That's the whole trick; leave them alone.

Now, if you were the *worst* parent in the world, you would do that *automatically*. You'd hear your infant cry and just disregard it. If, however, you're a halfway reasonable person, you run to their side and do whatever it takes to get them to sleep. You make sure they're fed, changed, comfortable, warm-but-not-too-warm, cozy, read to, sung to, patted, rocked, cuddled—do every trick in the book.

But not this guy's book. Here's a book, written by a medical doctor, a highly regarded professional pediatrician, that says, "No, don't do that. Just walk away. They'll stop eventually."

Now, our son had developed a particularly ambitious routine. He went down every night at about 8:00 P.M. and was up at 5:30 the next morning, but had several shows in between, customarily at 10:30, 1:30, 3:15, 4:00, and 4:40. Seven shows a night, my son was basically Vaudeville with Diapers. So we decided this hard-nosed approach was just what we needed. (The other option— shooting ourselves—seemed ultimately unreasonable.)

So we put the young prince to bed, tucked him in, sang to him, and started to sneak quietly away from his crib. Before we got to the door, he started to wail. We looked at each other—"You've *got* to be strong, soldier."

The book says you're supposed to let them cry for *five minutes,* then you can pat them a little bit.

I didn't last long.

"I'm going in."

"Don't."

"But he's crying."

"I know, but the book said . . ."

"I don't care about the book, he's crying!"

"If we don't do it, we're going to be his slaves for the rest of our lives. Do you want that?"

"No, but—"

"Okay, so let's wait."

As he continued to cry, we sat on the floor just outside his door and stared at our watches.

"Is it five minutes yet?"

"No."

"How long has it been?"

"Eleven seconds."

"Can't be."

"Twelve seconds, now."

My son was no doubt thinking, "Where are those two? . . . They always come when I cry . . . Maybe I'm not crying loud enough . . . Let me try *this*: 'WWWWAAAAAAAAAHHHH!!!' "

Miraculously, we made it to five minutes, then went in, calmed him down, proved to him that we hadn't left the country, and once he'd stopped crying, walked away again—this time for *six* minutes.

He cried as loud as a person that size is physically able to. We sat outside the door biting our knuckles.

"I hate this."

"I know. Me, too."

"How long has it been?"

"Forty-one seconds."

"LIAR."

"I swear to you—it's not yet a minute."

.   .   .

When his six minutes of prescribed misery was up, we went in again, calmed him down, assured him that his Mommy and Daddy were there for him for always and ever, no matter what . . . and as soon as he bought it, ran away again.

If you get to the point of making him cry for seven and then eight minutes in a row—and what parent wouldn't be proud of that?—then you're supposed to go into their room, but *not touch them.*

This was *more* torture.

"We see you crying, we know what you want, and we'd love to give it to you, but sadly, we're not allowed."

Back in the hall, now a solid forty-five minutes into this sadistic and as of this point *wildly ineffective* discipline, we sat on the floor, in tears, arms wrapped around our knees, rocking gently back and forth and cursing this freak of a doctor who had written the book. The reality is we were *physically restraining ourselves* from comforting the only person we loved this much, the only person who will ever need us this much, the only one who gives us the wonderful feeling of *being* needed this much, denying ourselves the joy of being able to instantly and thoroughly put another person at peace by merely showing up and being who we are . . . all of that we were willing to forgo just so we could see if the $12.95 we spent on the stupid book was worth it.

Our son, whose face was by now caked in dried-up tears and assorted nosey fluids, had come to a new understanding.

"Well, this changes everything. The one thing I knew was that if I needed anything, I could count on *them*. Especially *her*. But I see now I was wrong. I am alone in this world, and I will never trust anyone again. Ever. WWWWAAAAAHHHHHHHHHHHH!"

Little did he know how close by we were, or how miserable we were ourselves. As we sat there not lifting a finger to help, I wondered if I went through this when *I* was a baby. All those times I cried, were my parents really there but deliberately not letting me know it? Did they really have the solution to my happiness but for some reason resist the urge to give it to me?

And if so, how long did that last?

When I was seven, were they still outside my door, withholding the very things I wanted?

"Son, we know you want the Rock 'Em Sock 'Em Robots, and the Secret Avenger Espionage Attaché Case with retractable water pistols and three-way walkie-talkie set . . . and in fact we have it *right here*. We bought it, but we're not going to let you have it. And by the way, that girl you like in arithmetic class? We have her here, too. Right outside the door. But we read this book that said you can't have her either."

So we made a compromise. He could come sleep in our bed, but he couldn't nurse. We didn't realize immediately *how* monumentally stupid this was. It was roughly the same as inviting a twelve-year-old to a video arcade and locking up the quarters. But we had to break him of his nasty habits.

So he cries and cries. And he cries even more.

"So, what exactly is the plan again? We just don't feed him, and he'll stop crying?"

"Yeah."

Beat.

"Doesn't seem to be working."

It is now *four-oh-eight* in the morning and we've all slept a total of nine minutes, none of them consecutive. As he cries, we pat him on the back lovingly, hoping to convince him that these pats and the incessant "shhusshes" we're both supplying are somehow *better* than the sweet nectar he craves.

"We understand you're hungry, but in the long run, this will serve you better. This will build character." Of course he's thinking, "I don't want character, I want milk."

It wasn't long before I turned to my wife and said, "I will give you a thousand dollars right now to put your breast in his mouth. That's one thousand dollars, American. I will go to the bank right now and withdraw a stack of twenties if you just put an end to this . . ."

When bribery failed, I started attacking the very principles we had both signed off on.

"Come on, so he breast-feeds through college, that's nothing to be ashamed of."

"Do you want to keep waking up in the middle of the night forever?"

"No, but—"

"Well, how else is he going to learn?"

"I don't know, but—"

"Shh, here, pat him for a while—I gotta go eat some protein."

So now it's four-fifteen in the morning, I'm lying in bed awake, halfheartedly patting my son's back, wishing I was asleep, while my son is lying next to me, wishing someone would feed him and stop patting him on the back.

Trying to think of some way to soften this for him, to look at this in a positive light, I said, "You see, Son, the thing you have to learn is, sometimes, in life, you don't always get what you want . . . Sadly, I'm forty years older than you and still fighting it, too . . . But, if you could embrace this now, then by the time you're my age, you'll be a lot better off . . . although you'll probably have kids who won't let *you* sleep . . . so don't even listen to me, because I'm tired and I don't know what I'm saying."

And with my wife in the kitchen, the two pinheads lie in bed grappling with the cold fact that What We Have is, at least for the time being, not going to be What We Want, but instead—This.

Veteran Moms

When people talk about wanting to "have children someday," what they really mean is that they want *babies*. Nobody wants an angry adolescent. Nobody wants an obnoxious seven-year-old trying to wear out dirty words they just learned in school that day. What they really want is cute, adorable babies who love you and need you. The bad stuff is just the price you agree to pay for having the good stuff.

Which explains why mothers of fourteen- and fifteen-year-olds are ferociously drawn to babies. Having given birth, they know the joys: the velvet skin, the sweet buttermilk breath, the sparkling eyes, the look of longing that only you can fulfill. But these are all a vague memory now, buried beneath the tedium and torture of the more recent years. These women have needs. They need to hold little babies, and they need to do it soon. And *these* are the people you want to seek out at parties.

I'm telling you, these ladies are so anxious to get their hands on your baby, you're guaranteed all the quality child-free time you want. Because sometimes things you used to take for granted—like eating with two hands, or sipping a cocktail without twenty-two pounds of Small Person pinching your throat—can be an unthinkable luxury.

And you don't even have to ask; they volunteer. More than volunteer—they *beg*. You could be standing there, doing absolutely fine, and they'll say, "You know, if you'd like a break, I'll be happy to hold your baby for you for a while . . ."

And you think they're just flattering you, so you smile politely and say, "Thanks."

But ten minutes later, they swoop back in.

"I know you said 'no' before, but I just wanted to remind you, if you change your mind, I'd be more than happy to take over for a while . . ."

"Thanks."

"No, seriously, if you want a break, or think you might feel like one soon, or that maybe later, during the night, you might begin to think you feel like possibly thinking about a break, or you're going out of town in the near future, I'd be more than happy to take your baby for a while . . ."

They're so sincere and passionate, it's easy to forget that

what's fueling the craving is, "My own kids have sucked the very life out of me. I need something joyful, and I need it now! Help me, please."

But it's actually a win-win situation: You get your arms free for half an hour and they have a reason to live.

And this is all just one more piece of proof that life has changed. I used to walk into a party and scan the room for attractive single women. Now I look for women to hold my baby so I can eat potato salad sitting down.

My wife and I even load the dice in our favor now— we make sure the kid is up and looking extra-cute and needy. Maybe even spread some applesauce across his chin, so even if they don't see the baby, they can smell him coming around the corner. It's a whole scam. A ruse. I feel like one of those lotharios who prey on the recently widowed.

"Who here has a void within them, a longing, a sadness, an emptiness unsated for so long that I can manipulate their weakness to my own gain? Who will it be, girls? . . . Will it be . . . you?"

"Oh, is that your baby?"

"Why, yes, it is."

"He's just adorable . . ."

"Well . . ."

"You know, if you feel like taking a br—"

"Here."

They don't even finish their sentence anymore.

"Here you go, walk around, enjoy the baby . . . Now, where'd the guy go with the potato salad?"

"Yes, but Can He Do *This*?"

My wife and I were walking our child in his stroller through the park when we came upon another young couple with child in stroller.

"Cute baby," the woman said.

"Thanks. Yours, too," we replied.

Then the moms got down to business.

"How much weight did you gain?" she says.

In these conversations, someone always gets hurt.

"You gained *four* pounds? . . . Really . . ."

The instinct seems to be to fib *down*, not *up*. If you actually put on thirty pounds, call it twenty. Piled on forty to forty-five? Admit to thirty.

The more clever women, however, realize that it's to their advantage to say they gained more than they did, because it gives them the biggest leeway when answering the next question:

"How long did it take you to lose it?"

"Well, I still have some to get rid of. Sure, it was twenty-three years ago, but bear in mind, I put on a hundred eighty-seven pounds."

Throughout pregnancy, it's a challenge to avoid becoming too competitive. *After* the kid arrives, however, it's impossible. You do it uncontrollably. The moment you see another child, the race is on: Whose kid is cuter? Who's growing more? Whose kid is using both hands the way the experts say they should? Who's talking, who's not talking? Who's talking in sentences, who's making obscure literary references . . . ?

And again the accepted convention is: Lie. For all the sharing and being open and vulnerable, the truth is that all new parents are Big Fat Liars.

We lie about things that don't even mean anything. Like Sleeping Through the Night. You wouldn't think your newborn baby's ability to sleep or *not* sleep consecutive hours would be potential grounds for ridicule. But you'd be wrong.

"Our daughter came home from the hospital, and from that night forward, she slept perfectly. Went down at eight-thirty, woke up the next morning at nine."

Lies, lies, and more lies. Because if you told the truth, it might make *you* look bad. If your baby doesn't sleep through the night, it's a cultural stigma. It's like *The Scarlet Letter*—where the "A" stands for "We're still Awake, thank you very much." So even if you both have bags under your eyes the size of steamer trunks—lie.

"Well, yes, last night she did get up seven times, but only because there was a fireworks display across the street and construction on her crib . . ."

"Well, that explains it then."

"Yes, because otherwise, she sleeps exactly like however the books say she should be sleeping . . . and, frankly, a little better than yours."

Why do we play this game of parental one-upmanship? One word: Fear. We're all secretly afraid that our child might be even one micro-measurement less than "Perfect." Even if we're safely inside that generally wide and flexible normal range, it doesn't matter; if somebody's child is doing something our child isn't, we get nervous. Our kid has to be at least as Perfect as their kid. (If they turn out to be a tad *more* Perfect than their kid, even better.)

Of course, we don't want our child to be *too* ahead. A three-month-old doing advanced calculus in the crib is freakish, and you run the risk of them being officially labeled "Circus Act."

And surely you don't wish ill on somebody else's kid, either. You want to all be in the same ball park, with your kid sitting in slightly better seats.

Does This Come
with Puppies Instead
of Clowns?

If "cool" is measured by how little we care what others think of us, then babies are the coolest people on the planet.

There are no apologies or disclaimers in Babyland.

You never hear a baby say, "I just had garlic bread, so forgive me . . ." Or, "You know I'm still a little sweaty from racquetball, so don't hug me . . ." Hell, they'll wear a pantsful of lunch and sit right down to dinner. These guys just don't care.

Can you imagine walking into a room with a thing coming out your nose the size of a corn muffin and not caring? And then even expect people to pick you up and hug you? No. But for babies, it's not a problem. I myself would pay to be that cool.

This wonderful sense of confidence is particularly evident when it comes to their clothes. We dress babies up with some genuinely stupid apparel, and they just roll with it. They don't know what's on them, and they don't care.

There are two basic types of baby clothes: the "little adult" look and the "Look at me, I'm a cartoon" look. The first approach tries to disguise the fact that the subject is only twenty-three inches high—little tiny suits that make your child look like a ventriloquist's dummy, pint-sized jeans with back pockets, as if a four-month-old is going to go, "Oops, my wallet . . . I know I had it when I left the crib . . ."

I'm also a big fan of those hand-puppet-sized tank-top T-shirts. These are worn by those big beer-bellied babies you see every summer, sitting on the hood of a car, whistling at baby girls and spitting at traffic.

The vast majority of baby clothes, however, are of the brightly colored, animated-figure variety. Most have animals on them. It's some kind of federal regulation: All infant apparel must be flame retardant and feature a bear, a duck, or a rabbit.

It's a custom I don't quite understand. It's as if we're afraid that *without* the cute critters, babies alone are not quite cute *enough;* we need to underscore the point. Cute animals, cute baby. As if perhaps without these visuals, we wouldn't be sure they're babies.

"Look at that bald guy over there, drooling. He's so unbelievably short."

"Don't stare, that's just cruel."

"Oh, wait a minute, he's got Winnie-the-Pooh on his chest—he must be a baby. Never mind . . ."

And why bears? I'm stymied by the proliferation of bears. Bears are not that big a part of our culture; we don't see bears, we don't generally have them as pets. We don't even see *pictures* of bears on a day-to-day basis. Certainly not on clothing. I don't recall ever seeing an attorney walk into court in a bear-pattern suit and a honey-jar tie. But babies, we feel, should begin acclimating themselves to a potential world of bears as soon as possible.

It seems almost *all* of an infant's initiation to the world is via the animal kingdom. We're constantly showing them pictures of animals and quizzing them on what they say.

"What does the dog say? . . . 'Woof,' that's right. And the cow? 'Moo,' very good . . ."

Why are we wasting our time on this? Babies don't need to know this. Animals need to know this. And my guess is they already do. Actual animals rarely forget their lines. You're not going to see a baby zebra say "Moo," and have to be corrected by his mother.

"No, sweetie, that's cows. Now come on, talk regular."

I feel if you're going to put something in a human baby's brain, why not make it something they're going to use in life, like, "Pardon me, are you sure this is decaf?"

Or, more pressingly, "Who do I gotta suck up to to get some apple juice around here?"

Instead, we drill our kids on animal talk and pile on the animal clothes. Bear shirt, duck hat, rabbit pants— and the kids have no clue. They have no idea that, for our own amusement, they're walking around with their torsos covered in koala bears and their feet encased in rayon doggy-head slippers with tongues lapping. They never question. They never say, "Are you sure this sun bonnet in the shape of a possum doesn't make me look goofy?"

They simply don't care.

When it comes to fashion, newborns are basically human *props*—oblivious to the slogans and product endorsements, sentiments and attempts at humor stamped across their very bodies. Do you think they enjoy hawking the perennially not funny "Grandma-went-to-Atlantic-City-and-all-she-got-me-was-this-stupid-T-shirt" joke? I would doubt it. But they don't even know it's happening. They're miniature versions of the unlucky kid in junior high school with a "kick me" sticker on his back. They walk around simply for the entertainment of others.

The first time you step into a store's baby department alone is a frightening experience. It's like wandering into a ladies' bathroom, only cleaner, and without the thrill of the forbidden. Walking into a baby department just plain feels Wrong. In the past, I had only been in with my wife, and my job was to stand there while she bought something for someone else's baby and pretend that I had an opinion one way or another. That I could do.

But alone, and as an actual father, it's a bit daunting. In your gut you know you have no business being in there. Before I could steel myself to actually enter, I had to stand outside for a few minutes and just look. "Is there anyone in there I don't want to see?" "Am I going to be the only *guy* in there?" "Do other guys know how to do this any better than me?" "Are there women there who will mock me for my ignorance and incompetence?"

Finally, I took the plunge and walked in. It's a remarkably Non-Guy place to be. You're wandering aimlessly among pink and blue pajamas and party dresses and two-inch shoes. And clothes are not called what they are usually called. There are no "pants" or "shirts." All you have are shelves full of "onesies," "rompers," "snugglies," and "jumpers." These are not words I enjoy using. Most of my friends would not want to be overheard in public uttering the phrase, "Do you have this in a onesie?" or "Does this jumper come with puppies instead of clowns?"

And where do these terms come from? What kid actually "romps"? I had a very happy childhood, but cannot recall having at any point ever "romped." And if an infant can't even roll over, does he really need a "jumper"?

I say why not lessen the confusion and name the garment for what the kid is really doing at this stage.

"Excuse me, I'll take a 'Droolie,' one of those 'Lie-There-on-My-Backs' for my nephew, and one of these darling 'Make-in-My-Pants-and-Stare-at-Peoples,' in blue, if you have it."

I was wandering around for a few minutes when one of
the saleswomen came over.

"Can I help you?"

I felt like a twelve-year-old caught loitering in the dirty
magazine section of a newsstand.

"Just looking, thank you," I said.

The truth of the matter was I had never before needed
help in a store more than I did here. But it was a knee-
jerk response.

And as she turned away, I added, "Is this Sporting
Goods?"

I couldn't even tell you why I said that.

I wandered around by myself, and tried to figure it all
out alone.

I did learn a few things. For example, in the world of
baby finery, the French seem to be industry giants. Not
that the clothes are necessarily better, but they prey on our
sense of cultural inferiority—our belief that our children
are somehow more sophisticated if there's a French phrase
scribbled across them. Apparently, there's a line of clothes
called "Petite Toilette" that has as its logo a little baby
squatting. I couldn't understand why they would want to
put forth that particular image, or, for that matter, name
the whole company "Small Bathroom." I later found out
from a French mom that in this case, the word "toilette"
refers to a *procedure*. It's the *bathing* of the baby, and the
"petite" specifies it as not a complete head-to-toe bath
but rather a localized cleansing of the baby's bottom.

And that's when I realized how clever the French

are. In English, nobody would ever buy pajamas called "Just Wash My Ass." You're not going to drop twenty bucks for a pair of shorts that say, "No soap on my chest, please." But in French, it just sounds special, doesn't it?

Walking around the store, I realized that even just *handling* baby clothes among strangers makes you feel vulnerable. If you pick something up and simply consider it, you might as well be wearing the thing yourself, that's how dopey you feel. A grown man holding up pants the size of pliers going, "Yes, I admire *these*. I think this would be just the thing I'm looking for." It's just odd.

Having never bought clothes for a person this small, I discovered that one of the challenges is *translating* the sizes. Your old tricks of holding a shirt up to yourself or finding a woman roughly the size of your wife and eyeballing a dress against her no longer work. Suddenly, you're alone, holding a tiny pair of pajamas up to your neck to see how far down they dangle. You walk around the store, waltzing a snuggly to see if it feels like anything familiar.

"Let's see, if the top of these pajamas are at my neck, and the booties reach my sternum, that should fit my kid just fine."

And they don't have the customary Small, Medium, and Large. Instead, you're forced to calculate everything in terms of months: three to six months, eighteen to twenty-four . . . and my personal favorite, zero to three. That's the size you get if you're zero old. Is there anything that wouldn't fit someone who's zero? That's really just about as young as you could be.

"How old are you?"

"Nothing."

I have several problems with this "months" thing.

First of all, it's too much math. Up to a year, I suppose this system makes sense, but seventeen months, twenty-two months? Who wants to divide by twelve?

Then, in addition to dividing, you have to multiply, because they tell you you're supposed to buy everything twice as big as what it says. (Which, by the way, would mean that "0 to 3 months" fits *nobody*. Even twice zero is zero. These are clothes for kids in utero, or, at most, driving home from the hospital.)

Of course, sizing clothes by age could be fun if they applied it to adults.

"I need to buy a shirt for my husband. He'll be forty-six in March."

"Play it safe. Get him something for a ninety-two to a hundred-year-old."

As I wandered around the store, I did notice other fathers, equally lost and confused. All with the same sense of discomfort. You would think we might bond over our shared predicament. Reach out to one another in support. But in truth we're too embarrassed. We look away, and if we do accidentally make eye contact, we quickly glance at our watches, tap our feet, and look annoyed, as if we're thinking, "My wife said she'd meet me here twenty minutes ago . . . Where is she?"

Finally, the saleswoman comes around again.

"Are you sure I can't help you?"

A few of the other dads look my way. I think, "Me? Need help? Just because I'm standing in the middle of a department store with a pair of clown pajamas hanging from my neck trying to perform eighth-grade math in my head on forty-five minutes of sleep?"

I respond, "I'm fine, really . . ."

But before she gets away, I quietly follow her and ask, "Um, do you double the size or halve the size?"

She looks at me compassionately and says, "Why don't you just tell me what you need."

The eyes of the other dads are all upon me. I look at my watch. I've been in the baby department for an hour and a half and so far I've got nothing but a Yankee cap that would fit an orange.

"All right," I say. "I need a romper, a jumper, some bunting, and a onesie."

"How big is your child?"

"Smaller than you, bigger than your purse . . . See that stuffed dog? About like that."

"I'll get right on it."

"And one more thing . . ."

"Yes?"

"I prefer puppies to clowns."

"I'll do my best."

As she leaves, I try to make myself invisible to the gazing eyes of the other men. I feign an intense interest in a pair of *Hunchback of Notre Dame* slippers. But out of the corner of my eye, I see the other dads looking at me. One by one, they approach. I fear this might be like one of those marine hazing things where they tie me down in a crib and pummel me with knotted-up rompers.

The first guy comes right up to me. I tense. He looks me in the eye and says, "Man . . . that took guts."

"What?"

"The way you asked that lady for help. That was really something."

The guy actually admired me.

How's that for irony? You spend your whole life trying to get "guy respect." And how do I get it? Buying little pajamas with fuzzy feet.

Elephants Never Forget

"Wow."

"What?"

"Is he still sleeping?"

"Yeah . . . oh my God . . . he slept through the night . . ."

"That means *we* slept through the night."

"Geez . . . I feel terrific."

"Me, too . . . Hey—"

"What?"

"You're attractive. I forgot."

"You're not so bad yourself."

"There's no reason we couldn't have sex here."

"None at all."

"How much time do you think we have?"

"I don't know—*go.*"

Swingers

It was in the midst of trying to invent a new and exciting activity for our little guy that we rediscovered the classic fun center of all time—the Playground. These little oases of activity that we've driven by for years and taken for granted, now, with a crabby youngster in the backseat, suddenly shimmer like Coke machines in a desert.

But they're not exactly the way I remember them. Like sandboxes, for example. When I was a kid, as best I can recall, sandboxes were just big enough to hold about a half dozen toddlers. Now they put sand throughout the entire surrounding area, so that grown-ups are walking around in sand, too. An enormous litter box for humans.

Maybe this is designed for those among us who find that having a child is not enough to reconnect to their own childhood. So, in addition to pushing yellow Mighty Mouse swings, they also need that mushy feeling underfoot. Whatever the reason, I don't like it. When you're forty, you shouldn't be walking around with sand in your shoes.

Having not been inside an actual playground for a few decades, I was surprised how vividly my own childhood memories came back. And not all of them pleasant. I had forgotten about the whole social component: the inter-acting with others, the animalistic "sniffing out" process that quickly makes friends or enemies.

As my little one was sitting in the swing, another kid— a stranger—waddled up and put his hands on my kid's swing. Maybe it wasn't exactly hostile, but it was certainly confrontational. There was a challenge in his walk, daring in his eyes . . . the kid spelled trouble. Granted, he was no more than eighteen months old, but I'm telling you, he had a swagger, an in-your-face quality not unlike a very small Joe Pesci.

Instantly, I remembered every bully that pushed me around, every punk that wandered in from another neighborhood just to play "keep-away" with my hat . . . It all came back.

But this time I was bigger.

I said, "Hey!"

A few parents turned. I was, after all, yelling at a baby. I softened my tone.

"I mean, hey, *Buckaroo*. What do you say you wait just a minute and then it'll be your turn on the swing."

But, as you can imagine, Joe Pesci is not someone who backs down easily. His fat little mitt remained right on my son's swing. Every cell in my body pulsated with the instinct to protect my cub. But since I am, after all, a civilized man, not to mention being someone's father, someone for whom I want to set an example, I tried to handle this diplomatically. I politely and calmly explained to the precious toddler the rules of sharing and playing nicely, while knowing full well that if he went ahead and actually *touched* my son, I would grab him by his tiny jacket and fling him like a discus. It had taken me only several decades to find that confidence. (Yes, it was with someone whose head didn't come up to my knee—but nonetheless . . .)

Still, Tough Guy, Jr., didn't budge. My son, sensing the tension in the air, the musky aroma of battle on the horizon, started to make that drama-award face that precedes a cry. It was just then that the thug's daddy appeared.

"Son," he said, "why don't you let the other little boy take his turn and then you can go?"

At which point, he smiled at me pleasantly and said, "Kids . . ."

I smiled back.

"Yeah, kids." Thinking, "Especially *your* kids."

Whether it was coincidence or genuine obedience, I don't know, but the hooligan retreated. He took his hands off the swing.

My son breathed a sigh of relief. Then the other kid

said, "Push?" My son looked at me, and I looked at him, equally confused.

"He wants to push your son," the father translated.

My jaw re-clenched.

"He wants to push my son?"

"On the swing, on the swing. He wants to push him on the *swing*."

"Oh."

I then realized that this standoff may very well have been for nothing. This kid just wanted to play.

"Do you want the little boy to push you?" I asked.

My son looked at me, looked at the kid, and then back to me, as if to say, "Yeah, why not." And the kid proceeded to gently, playfully push my son's swing for him. The other father and I breathed a sigh of relief, fully aware that only moments earlier, we had all stood on the brink of some very unfortunate hostilities. We both put away our protective armor, disengaged our animal instincts and painful childhood histories, and attempted to talk about hockey.

Once you spend enough time in a playground, you'll notice this is definitely not a place where *single* people go. And with reason. For one thing, there are very few other single people for them to meet there. And even if a single person met another single person in a playground, there are very few dating amenities. There's no cappuccino counter, no cocktail area, no bookstore to aimlessly browse through. Unless you hope to make an impression with your monkey-bars agility, the playground is not a place for you.

No, the playground is where parents and children go. And in case you still have doubts about your new identity, there's nothing like pushing your own kid on a swing to make you realize you're no longer Not a Parent.

Because there was a time, after my son was born, when I still periodically considered myself Not a Parent. In my mind, "parents" were those other people. Older. More settled. I was simply a young guy with a young wife, and it so happens, I happened to have with me—very often—this cute little guy with the tiny Yankee hat. That didn't necessarily make me a "Parent."

But one day, with my son ensconced in his favorite swing, I rhythmically pushed him back and forth across the clouds, and it started to sink in. I began to feel—and very happily so—a part of the vast continuous cycle of people who pushed their kids in swings just like this. I remembered the black-and-white photo I have of my parents pushing me in a swing, my head cupped firmly in a mandatory woolen hat with earflaps. And I realized that my mother and father must have been, more or less, what I am now: somebody who just got a kid. No longer kids themselves, not yet the softer, rounder people in the color pictures that came afterward. They were just making their way from Then to Later.

Now it *is* later, and I'm doing the pushing, and my son is the one wearing dopey hats and squealing with delight.

We all just change positions; we start as the Ones Who

Get Pushed, and we become the Ones Who Push. The only thing that stays the same is the swing.

And as my little boy was flying through the air, screeching with joy, I felt satisfied that somehow he was making memories, too, and someday, he'd be pushing someone else in an equally small hat.

And in the End . . .

I was in the middle of changing a diaper when the phone rang. I picked it right up.

An interesting shift had taken place in our phone habits, I noticed. Since becoming parents, we were almost always too busy or too tired to talk to anyone on the phone, but because we never wanted the ringing to wake up or disturb the boy, we invariably grabbed every call on the first ring. As a result, we not only spoke to many more people than we did when we let our answering machine do its job, but we also compiled a list of People-We-Spoke-to-Briefly-and-Told-Them-We'd-Call-Them-Right-Back that will take us at least fifteen years to contend with.

"Changing table, may I help you?"

"How's my little boy?"

"You know, Mom, I'm actually all grown up now, so—"

"Not you, your son. How's my little boy?"

"Oh . . . him. He's really good. Hold on, I'll put him on . . . Here, it's Grandma. Say hi to Grandma."

Nothing.

Grandma coaxed.

"Hellooooooo . . . Hiya, sweetie pie . . . Hello . . . Helllooooooo . . . Helllloooow, sugarplum . . ."

My son stared at the receiver and then put the mouthpiece all the way into his mouth. (Hence the term "mouthpiece.")

"Hi, sweetie, it's your Grandma. Don't you want to say hi to your Grandma?"

"Aaaarlrrrah."

"Did you hear that, Mom?"

"Aaaarlrrrah aaarrrgah."

"There, he said it again."

"What?"

"That was him saying, 'Grandma.' "

"Really?"

"I swear. That's how he says, 'Hi, Grandma, I'm looking forward not only to seeing you tomorrow but also taking my very first airplane ride and potentially catching one of seventeen thousand diseases from everybody on the plane because the airlines keep circulating the same old air and blowing germs right on your head.'"

"I never should've sent you that article."

"Yeah, well, it's too late now. Listen, I got to get off, the baby's hungry."

Nobody argues with that excuse.

"Okay. Have a safe trip. And take a sweater."

"Ma . . ."

"Not for you, for the boy."

"I will."

"See you tomorrow."

When we got on the plane, I finally understood why they let people with small children get on board first. It's not because you need more time to put things away; it's because they want to spare you all those dirty looks. When we stepped onto the plane, my wife holding our son, me lugging three bags, a collapsible stroller, a car seat, a video camera, and a panda bear the size of Buddy Hackett, every person on the plane looked up with an expression that said, "Please, whatever you do, don't sit near us."

There's a palpable discrimination you face when you travel with an infant. Like hotels that happily took our reservations until we mentioned we needed a crib.

"A crib? Why did you say 'crib'?"

"Because we're circus people and we're traveling with a seal. Whadaya think—we have a baby."

"Oh, I'm sorry, we don't accept babies."

"What do you mean you don't 'accept' babies? There's nothing to accept. This is not some crazy kid running around vandalizing your ice machine. This is an infant. And not just any infant—this is *our* infant. Perhaps the sweetest boy working the country today. What kind of sick people are you?"

Never mind the fact that less than a year ago I myself would call up hotel managers and ask them to relocate the people with the screaming kids to another side of town because my wife and I—"regular people"—were trying to get some rest.

Settling into her seat, my wife began to breast-feed our son to relieve his ear pressure during takeoff (which, I understand, hands-down beats the hell out of chewing gum).

"Honey," she said, "could you get his jacket? I think it's in the canvas bag"—which I had just finished cramming into the overhead compartment, behind the impossible-to-collapse stroller, two puffy down jackets, and our four-hundred-pound diaper bag.

I hoisted myself up, gathering a lap full of stuffed animals and assorted containers of half-chewed oranges, gummed bananas, and sampled-but-rejected soggy crackers and dumped them on my seat. Yanking open the compartment, I was hit in the eye with a rubber duck. As I swatted him away, I noticed—directly across the aisle—a young couple who'd been watching the whole show.

"How are ya?" I mumbled politely, knowing full well what they were thinking.

"Our lives are *sooo* wonderful and simple and carefree, and we're so much happier than you poor slobs with your baby." That's what they were thinking—I just knew it. But I was on to them.

"Have any kids yourself?" I asked, like I didn't already know.

"No," the guy said, "but we're thinking about it."

A short while later, somewhere over the Great Lakes, I imagine, I had my son in my lap and was reading him one of his favorite books. When you're very young, by the way, your favorite book isn't necessarily the one with the best story or even the prettiest pictures. It's the one whose pages taste best. The book that goes easy on your gums is a great read.

"I enjoy Faulkner's storytelling, but his novellas tend to cut me in the roof of the mouth. Dickens, on the other hand, soft and nice."

As I read my boy his book, and he chewed on the chewiest chapters, I noticed the couple looking at me, but now a little less condescendingly.

"He's a beautiful boy," the guy said.

"Oh, thanks," I acknowledged politely.

"Is this your first child?"

"Yup . . . first one . . ."

My son, who must have sensed that he was not only the object of discussion but also the floor model for this couple on the brink of their big decision, took the book out of his mouth and offered it to them, while smiling one of his hard-to-argue-with killer smiles.

They both melted. The woman reached over to caress my son's cheek.

"I could eat you up with a big spoon," she cooed.

"What's it like?" the guy asked.

"What's *what* like?" I said, making him work for it a little.

"Kids. Having kids. Is it good? I mean, we want to have kids, but everybody says it changes your whole life and everything. So, I was just wondering if it's really true. If, y'know, . . . is it good?"

Having been there myself, I knew how vulnerable they were. I could make 'em or break 'em. I turned to my wife.

"What do you think, honey?"

"About what?"

"These nice people are thinking about having a baby."

"Oh," she said. "Good for you guys."

Then turning back to me, she said, "Well, that's a darn good question. What do you think we should tell them?"

We looked at each other and smiled. What should we tell them? Should we tell them it's the hardest and scariest thing any sane people could ever do? Do we let them know that having a child drains you, depletes you, exhausts you, and frustrates you until you end up hiding in your car whimpering like a puppy?

How can you explain that having a child drives you as far apart as you've ever been, yet it draws you together more deeply and magically than ever before—all at the same time?

That after you've both spent an aggravating, mind-numbing hour-and-a-half rocking, walking, patting, *begging* your child to sleep, there's nothing you'd rather do than spend the next hour and a half together, watching this angel sleep.

How can you explain that in the midst of a cranky discussion over who's not "being supportive" of whom, you notice how adorably and hilariously your child is eating a bowl of spaghetti, and suddenly all the things you fret about just don't matter?

You can't.

I turned to the couple and said, "Yeah, it's good. You'll see."

They nodded and drifted into their own conversation.

I held my boy's face in my hands and planted a juicy kiss on his cheek. I leaned over and kissed my wife, too.

"What did we do before we had this boy?" I asked.

"*That* . . . ," she said, smiling at the other couple.

I couldn't believe how a handful of months could obliterate everything that had come before.

"But now we're *this*," she said.

Our son sat in his mother's lap, one hand wrapped around her fingers, one hand on my nose.

"You know what?" I said. "I like this better."

Acknowledgments

A huge thank you to my friend Brad "Zippy" Kesden, whose smart, funny brains and invaluable input helped me make this book a lot better than I was planning to.

Also to my Assistant with a Capital "A," Meredith Kadlec, for making sure I never accidentally deleted the whole thing.

Big thanks to Arthur "Don't Worry, You Can Take as Long as You Want" Spivak.

And to the incomparable Rob "But I Need It Now" Weisbach for his unwavering confidence and support.

Thanks to Michael James for keeping those sandwiches coming.

Thanks also to Marc Jaffe.

And, of course, Paula and the Prince.